The Great Divide

Also by Gary Ferguson

Hawks Rest: A Season in the Remote Heart of Yellowstone

Shouting at the Sky: Troubled Teens and the Promise of the Wild

The Yellowstone Wolves: The First Year

The World's Great Nature Myths

Through the Woods: A Journey Through America's Forest
(The Sylvan Path)

The Great

Divide

THE ROCKY MOUNTAINS IN THE AMERICAN MIND

Gary Ferguson

W. W. NORTON & COMPANY

NEW YORK • LONDON

For information about permission to reproduce selections from this book,
write to Permissions, W. W. Norton & Company, Inc.,
500 Fifth Avenue, New York, NY 10110

Manufacturing by The Courier Companies, Inc.
Book design by BTD NYC
Production manager: Amanda Morrison

Library of Congress Cataloging-in-Publication Data
Ferguson, Gary, 1956–
The great divide : the Rocky Mountains in the American mind / Gary Ferguson.— 1st ed.
p. cm.
Includes bibliographical references and index.
ISBN 0-393-05072-6
1. Rocky Mountains Region—History. 2. Natural history—Rocky Mountains Region.
3. Rocky Mountains Region—Social life and customs. 4. Rocky Mountains Region—
Public opinion. 5. Public opinion—United States. I. Title.
F721.F46 2004
978—dc22

2004002566

W. W. Norton & Company, Inc., 500 Fifth Avenue, New York, N.Y. 10110
www.wwnorton.com

W. W. Norton & Company Ltd., Castle House, 75/76 Wells Street, London W1T 3QT

1 2 3 4 5 6 7 8 9 0

for Jane

Contents

Acknowledgments

MY SPECIAL THANKS TO AN EXCEPTIONAL group of archivists, librarians, and researchers, including George Miles of Yale University, Erin Royston of Harvard, and independent researcher Judy McHale. Also to the talented and dedicated staff of the University of Wyoming, the Denver Public Library, and the Buffalo Bill Historical Center.

The Great Divide

Introduction

Women Hunters, 1880

PHOTOGRAPHER UNKNOWN

Physicians and social pundits of the early twentieth century remained convinced that women should avoid strenuous pursuits. Women thought otherwise. As the century unfolded, an increasing number headed to the Rockies; there they engaged in a host of vigorous activities, including hunting elk, mule deer, moose, and antelope.

FOR MOST OF OUR NATION'S HISTORY, writes celebrated scholar Henry Nash Smith, Americans defined themselves "not by streams of influence from the past, not by a cultural tradition nor by its place in a world community, but by a relation between man and nature." More specifically, Smith goes on to say, by the bond "between American man and the American West." Of all the sweeping, sunblistered uplands tossed across this American West, few have sustained that relationship better, have been more full of both wonder and intrigue, than the 1,100-mile stretch of high country running from the pinyon-juniper foothills of Santa Fe north into Colorado and Wyoming, through Montana to the massive turrets of Glacier National Park. The Rocky Mountains.

At a bare minimum, there remains in this range today a clear and present startle factor. Here is life hanging by its toes at the edge of oblivion: steep cirque basins in Rocky Mountain National Park and the Wind River Range, in the heart of every summer smeared with strawberry-colored blooms of monkey flower, the orange and raspberry of paintbrush, the lavender of elephant head. Along the entire crest of the range on July afternoons comes lightning and sleet and hail, often in helpings big enough to terrify anyone caught above tree line. Winter snows pile to depths of twenty, even thirty feet—sometimes at a rate of six feet per storm. Windchills of sixty and seventy degrees below zero are common, freezing skin in a matter of seconds.

Hardly a story is told of this region in which the land isn't cast as a major character. Over the course of two hundred years these river bends, box canyons, and reaches of tundra have become dog-eared pages of a history both real and imagined, sparking in visitors and longtime residents alike flashes of dramatic notions about the past. Standing today at 10,000 feet on Montana's East Rosebud Plateau, for example, easily visible to the north some sixty miles away, are the abrupt walls of the Crazy Mountains; meanwhile, well to the southeast is the Pryor Range, an island of tilted stone rising from the grassy skin of the prairie. To members of the Crow tribe this hundred-mile arc of the horizon continues to bring to mind notions of Plenty Coups, the celebrated leader who in the mid-1800s, as a boy on a vision quest high in the Crazy Mountains, received one of the most highly regarded, disturbing visions of his time. The great herds of buffalo will disappear, he told his people, declaring it well before most would have believed such a thing possible—to be replaced by a slower, squatter domesticated beast that would pour in by the thousands.

In that same vision Plenty Coups saw himself enter the earth from the neck of the Crazies only to rise up out of the ground far to the southeast at a sacred spring, near a cottonwood at the edge of the Pryors. There he glimpsed himself as an old man sitting on the porch of a log cabin, a stone's throw from that sacred tree. All of which came true. The cabin he lived in still stands, at the edge of a reservation surrounded by cattle ranches. The springs of his dreams flow nearby, used even now by Crow traditionalists to break their fast after the rigors of the annual sun dance. Even the progeny of the cottonwood are here—beautiful, if on some days somewhat solemn, their branches whispering toward a run of graves scattered on a nearby ridge, most filled with people killed long ago by smallpox.

Still others might look out from this same perch on the East Rosebud Plateau to the northwest, toward an enormous sprawl of wilderness out of sight—the lands of the Bob Marshall Wilderness, hovering in the heart of a mountain complex embracing as much land as Rhode Island and Delaware combined. Meadows by the hundreds. Limestone cliffs a thousand feet high. That place the Blackfeet came to in the middle of the eighteenth century, pushing weaker tribes before them, establishing in fifty years a territory that stretched from Saskatchewan to southern Montana; the strongest, most aggressive power on the northwestern plains.

Turning to the south, we find a land rolling into Wyoming in a state of constant outrage. Especially prominent are the staggering walls of Wyoming's Absaroka, Teton, and Wind River Ranges, overlapping at the edges, pushing moisture-laden clouds from the Pacific to loose their cargoes on the Great Divide. High country in spades. Within the borders of the Shoshone National Forest alone lie a whopping 156 glaciers, more than in any other region of similar size in the continental United States. A stomping ground for grizzlies and mountain lions, wolves and beaver, the latter keeping house on a thousand quiet streams meandering through tilted meadows, much as they did nearly two hundred years ago, in the heyday of the fur trade.

Barely south of the Wind River Range the mountains make an easy tumble toward South Pass, for twenty years the primary route across the Rockies for travelers on the Oregon Trail. Today the route is windswept, lonely, a few old men walking the wagon ruts with metal detectors, conjuring visions of wagons and oxen and pioneers. From there the Great Divide loses its stature for a time, splitting in two and drifting in low ridges to form a circle around the Red Desert. Sporting the largest unfenced region in the continental United States, this is as close to the middle of nowhere as you can get—a land of alkali-choked nooks and ravines that offer no hint of the explosion of high country farther to the south. Here is home to the largest migratory game herd in the continental United States—a herd of pronghorn, commonly known as antelope, numbering close to fifty thousand animals. Thanks to the slow decomposition common to such arid climates, one has an almost palpable sense here of lives long vanished: ancient campsites littered with the bones of pronghorn; two-thousand-year-old panels of rock art; an enormous volcanic plug rising out of the desert—the Boar's Tusk—dark and still, nearly unchanged from when it was a sacred site of the Shoshone.

And then Colorado. The most expansive show of all, a fireworks of basalt and granite reaching from Denver 250 miles west nearly to the Utah border. To cross Colorado at nearly any latitude is to tumble into the Valhalla of the high country—fifty-four peaks soaring to heights above 14,000 feet, hundreds more only slightly lower. From the staggering tumble of horns and cirques and arêtes that make up Rocky Mountain National Park, to the bulwarks of the Maroon Bells, near Aspen, from the Spanish Peaks near Aguilar, to the dizzy heights of the Collegiate Range, across the Rio Grande and onto the remnant volcanic slopes of the San Juans. Assigned the task of designing the perfect reach of upland, most people would end up with something close to this. Continuing into New Mexico, the range narrows, cradled by a high, rolling savanna strewn with pinyon and juniper, rabbit brush and Gambel oak, splitting and finally all but disappearing in a desert tableland two hundred miles north of the Mexican border.

Little wonder millions of people still rubberneck through these parks and forests, clutching at their steering wheels on the canted roadways that sprawl across the tundra. National forests in the Colorado Rockies alone will this summer tally enough visitors to fill New York City ten times over. To the north, in Greater Yellowstone, hundreds of thousands of wildlife lovers will come again—including one especially passionate group that economists say will leave close to $25 million in local coffers for nothing more than the chance to glimpse a wild wolf. Even in the down times, the shoulder seasons, families across the nation will dial in the Discovery Channel, or Animal Planet, happy to watch otters doing belly rolls in the upper Colorado River, bighorn sheep tossing themselves down the frozen foothills of Wyoming's Wind River Range, or elk in Montana, pawing through crusted snow for bites of fescue and brome.

Yet despite our clear affection for this mountain range, few are aware of how the Rockies shaped, even expanded, the American imagination over some two hundred years. Like so much of the intermountain West, this is a land that on most days seems stuck in time, a jukebox stuffed with nineteenth-century frontier yarns, most of them written by a powerful group of Anglos obsessed with nationalism. The formal record of the Rockies is one of manly, blustering struggles in the high country in the name of gold and silver, of brutal battles between wealthy kingpins for control of the open range, of railroads commandeering more acreage than was distributed during the entire Homestead Act—the best and worst of it platted and sold for enormous profits to easterners desperate for a good dream.

Yet these mountains have also inspired far more brackish and poetic notions. While pioneers heading west in Conestogas often faced brutal circumstances, few met the Rockies with the kind of disgust or apprehension appropriate to a place routinely depicted as barren and dangerous— the entire territory, as one member of Congress put it, not worth a pinch of snuff. The range has not a single redeeming quality, claimed South Carolina senator George McDuffie, except perhaps as a potential barrier to protect Americans from foreign invaders: "If there was an embankment of only five feet to be removed, I would not consent to expend five dollars to remove that embankment to enable our population to go there." But pioneer diaries from the Rocky Mountain portions of the Oregon Trail are in most cases filled with awe and delight. Writing about the range in a letter to his wife in 1850, Pusey Graves tells of "a wildness, richness and grandeur that seemed to clothe the whole landscape. The beautiful pine trees which filled the air with aromatic fragrance, and the ten thousand flowers that were blooming all about me filling the mountain air with their unfolded treasures, the chatter of the blackbird and the sweet singing of the meadow lark . . . all this was indescribably grand and magnificent." Likewise Mrs. E. A. Hadley describes South Pass, at the very crest of the Rockies, as "the pleasantest place I have yet seen." Velina Williams, scribbling in her diary in 1853, waxes poetic about "the main chain of the Rocky Mountains to the north [of South Pass], with their snow-clad tops towering to a great height . . . truly grand and worth a journey across the plains."

The contrast between these two remarkably different perspectives—one revealing a hunger for paradise, the other a desperate urge to control it—also stands in sharp relief east of the Rockies, on the Great Plains. Traveling as part of one of the earliest government expeditions to the Rocky Mountains in 1824, Edwin James pronounced the prairies "a disgusting, horrible landscape." The entire midsection of the continent, he assured his readers, was nothing but a "great American desert"—a characterization that helped dry up government money for further explorations of the West for nearly twenty years. Horace Greeley, Daniel Webster, and Zebulon Pike were hardly any kinder. "What do we want with this vast tractless area," scoffed Webster, "this region of savages and wild beasts, of deserts, of shifting sands, and whirlwinds of dust, of cactus and prairie dogs? To what use could we ever hope to put these great deserts or these great mountain ranges, impenetrable and covered to their base with eternal snow?" Newspapers of the day stumping for manifest destiny took such loathing a giant step further, claiming we should settle the prairie quickly—not just because such landscapes would attract ruffians but because they would unleash barbaric urges even in civilized men, leading to unspeakable havoc on the frontier.

Once again, though, common travelers were enthralled by the Great Plains, casting them as a place where terror and beauty stood together—a fresh and stirring example of the sublime. "Alternately rolling and flat, having a rich soul," wrote future Oregon Supreme Court judge J. Quinn Thornton of the Kansas prairie. "The scenery of the country through which we passed during the day was in a high degree interesting and delightful, and more than compensated for the fatigue of travel; it seemed to give us a most delicious foretaste of the satisfaction we expected to enjoy in the subsequent portion of our journey, in which we anticipated seeing the grandeur of nature in all her wildest and most imposing aspects." U.S. Army soldier Phillip St. George Cooke writes in 1845 of dazzling sunrises on the Great Plains, of places where nature "has there assembled in the desert the admired features of her favorite regions: the contrast is delightful at meeting, painful at parting." Willa Cather, far from seeing the prairies as unleashing unholy behavior, found that such overwhelming exposure created in her neighbors a tendency to see daily life unmasked—things as they are, rather than as they should be.

The missing pieces of history in the great landscapes of the West are found most often in the experiences of nonpolitical travelers, artists, Native Americans and other minorities, as well as in the disaffected children of wealthy families from the eastern United States, England, and Europe. It's not that such travelers didn't come with agendas of their own. Yet their descriptions of the region are vastly more layered, more vigorous than the thin gruel offered up by politicians and religious leaders to fuel the engines of empire. Such writings are centered less on fear than on ideas of space and freedom and beauty. The very qualities that inspired farm and ranch families in the late 1800s to load up kids and sacks of potatoes in horse-drawn box wagons and drive three hundred, even five hundred miles for monthlong vacations in Yellowstone National Park. That led small groups of daring women to declare their independence by roaming the Rockies in Model T's. Or black men to escape racial intolerance long before the Civil War, trapping and working cattle, finding something close to equality on the banks of the upper Missouri River, in wind-shorn cow camps on the eastern slopes of Colorado.

Granted, the same high country that fed such ambitions

has for writers and artists alike been a constant source of sensationalism. Much of what's been written about this range is wrapped in enough gush to shame a pack of evangelists. Edward Abbey compared the feeling of seeing the Rockies to the rumblings brought on by his first love. Summing up his enthusiasm for an excursion on the upper Yellowstone, in Yankee Jim Canyon, Rudyard Kipling was reduced to a bumbling "Ye gods!" Traveling Colorado's famous Gold Camp Road, Teddy Roosevelt looked around, shook his head, and threw up his hands. "This is the view that bankrupts the English language." It was the Rockies that some critics had in mind when they stated that beautiful regions of the world rarely produce decent writers, leaving even the most talented too overwhelmed to create anything of value.

And yet much can be learned from their attempts. Julia Archibald Holmes, traveling through Colorado with her husband in 1858, became the first known woman to survey the surrounding countryside from the summit of Pikes Peak, having climbed there in moccasins and bloomers. "Nearly every one tried to discourage me from attempting it, but I believed that I should succeed," she writes in a letter to her mother, later published in the Lawrence, Kansas, *Republican*. And there a hint of what would soon become a common theme in the Rockies—namely, their use as a place for women of means to escape the chauvinistic ideals of nineteenth-century high society. Wishing she had the facility of a poet, Holmes goes on to give a stunning portrait of the mountain. She was taken aback by the clear streams "rushing, tumbling and hissing down over the rough mountain sides," as well as "tiny blue flowers most bewitchingly beautiful, children of the sky and snow." From the summit she relished the verdure of the plains, the windings of the Arkansas and its numerous tributaries—rugged peaks all around, an endless run of high country. All of this, she writes, sounding remarkably like her contemporary Ralph Waldo Emerson, "and everything on which the eye can rest, fills the mind with infinitude and sends the soul to God."

Likewise another woman, Isabella Bird, would fifteen years later make a rugged late-autumn climb to the top of 14,255-foot Longs Peak in Colorado, pronouncing it as not just the noblest peak in the Rockies but a place that in one's imagination is more than a mountain. "Uplifted above love and hate and storms of passion, calm amidst the eternal silences, fanned by zephyrs and bathed in living blue, peace rested for that one bright day. . . ."

The Rockies are as close as America has come to an archetypal landscape—a region that, although far removed from the core of society, reflected much about our most persistent longings. But then such has been the tradition of mountains. The Egyptians carried with them dreams of the sun god Ra, emerging each day from behind the mountain of the sunrise to begin his journey in the Menjet Boat across the Braque of Millions of Years, the vessel finally passing at sunset through a chain of mysterious peaks in the west. Alexander the Great, entering a palace in the high country, was reportedly granted by the resident mountain god access to the fortune-telling powers of the Tree of the Sun and Tree of the Moon. Or the Muslims, cherishing the peak known as Kaf, the mother of all mountains, meeting place of the visible and invisible, the mountain that nurtures every other range in the world through an intricate system of underground branches and veins.

Tales are told still of the Taoist immortals known as the Sien—literally "the men of the mountains"—while the emperor of China continues to give thanks for his dynasty to the five sacred mountains. Meanwhile the followers of Judaic and Christian traditions have never tired of recounting Isaiah's prediction that in the final days the Lord will "establish His house in the tops of the mountains, and all nations shall flow onto it." Sunday schools talk of Noah's ark running aground on the summit of Mount Ararat, of the prophet Elie achieving the miracle of rain on Mount Horeb. Christ is said to have showed himself to his apostles transfigured by the light of God atop Mount Tabor, and later to have risen into heaven from the Mount of Olives. Even the Garden of Eden was throughout the Age of Exploration thought to have survived the biblical flood, awaiting rediscovery in some unknown land atop a stray mountain. For the vast majority of the world's cultures the high country has at one time or another been portrayed as a refuge above the struggles and limits of the mundane world. Clearly the human spirit rises on images of ascent.

New York artist Frederic Remington summed it up

well when he explained that the highest value of a place like the Rockies was simply to remind us of the world that existed "beyond tasseled loafers, derby hats and mortgages bearing eight percent." Even that least of all nature boys, Sigmund Freud, speculated that such wild preserves served the same function for a culture that fantasy did for an individual. It wasn't that Freud thought people had to actually be in the wilderness (God forbid), only that they be able to envision it—not just in terms of inspiration or entertainment but as strange and outrageous, beautiful and frightening and full of mystery.

Fire, Ice, and a
Humorless God

The Grand Canyon of the Yellowstone (1893–1901)

THOMAS MORAN

Moran's great portrayal of the Yellowstone River, seen here from Artist's Point, was first shown at Clinton Hall in New York City to tremendous acclaim. Indeed, the artist became so firmly associated with the newly formed national park that he was sometimes referred to as Thomas "Yellowstone" Moran. Congress eventually acquired this work for the princely sum of $10,000.

STRETCHING FROM THE MEXICAN PLATEAU south of Santa Fe nearly to the southern reaches of Alaska—a north-south reach extending across a staggering thirty-four degrees of latitude, or nearly one-tenth of the circumference of the world—the Rocky Mountains cover some 300,000 square miles, making them by far the largest range in North America. Most of the great rivers of the continental West, including the Missouri, Rio Grande, Colorado, Columbia, Snake, and Arkansas, have their source in these peaks, more than a thousand of which soar to elevations above 10,000 feet. Roughly a quarter of the American water supply is fed by the watersheds of the Rockies; in Colorado alone the alpine tundra, which makes up only 3.5 percent of the state's landmass, produces fully 20 percent of the stream flows. While not as biologically diverse as warmer and wetter habitats, more than two thousand vascular plants are found in the forests, riparian zones, and tundra of the region, as well as roughly seventy-five mammals. Included in the mix are those stalwart symbols of the western wilderness—the grizzly, bison, elk, and wolf. In the northern reaches of the lower 48, the Greater Yellowstone ecosystem is now widely recognized as the largest intact ecosystem in the temperate world.

Living in the upper elevations of the Rockies calls for extraordinary survival strategies. At the highest points, far up on the tundra, vegetation is made up largely of cushion plants—matlike structures sporting tight folds of ground-hugging leaves. Such design not only lessons the abrading effect of mountain winds but allows the trapping of considerable heat, leaving temperatures inside the leaf mats as much as twenty degrees warmer than the surrounding air. While plants in lowland environments are not able to start growing roots until the temperatures reach the mid-forties, even the fifty-degree mark, tundra vegetation gets down to business as soon as the thermometer inches past freezing. Alpine flora are also far better at maintaining rapid respiration rates in cold weather than their lowland counterparts; this in turn allows them to store more sugars and starches in their underground root stems—vital for quick sprouting in a land where the growing season is barely ten weeks long.

Birds and animals, meanwhile, have tricks of their own. The white-tailed ptarmigan—out of a mere half dozen birds that breed and nest on the tundra, the only one to live here year-round—molts three different sets of feathers from winter to fall, including a heavy set for deep winter along its legs and feet, which leaves the birds from a distance looking as though they're wearing snowshoes and pantaloons. The jittery pika, or rock rabbit, spends the long days of summer cutting vegetation and drying it on rocks like so much hay, later stacking it in underground burrows to serve as dinner throughout the winter. There are no earthworms here, and much of the aeration of the soil comes from the tireless diggings of pocket gophers—an animal smaller than a hot dog bun yet, thanks to a set of large yellowish-orange incisors, able to excavate vast networks of burrows, moving several tons of soil in a single year. Likewise, since bees tend to lose their mobility at temperatures around fifty degrees, much of the pollination at high elevations occurs by way of flies. Those bumblebees who do find their way up here can be spotted on many mornings stumbling across the ground waiting for their wings to warm, looking like hungover sailors. Larval stages, including those of butterflies, which at lower altitudes last for roughly a month, can on these mountaintops extend for years.

There are countless examples of plants whose march to colonize these mountains ends in vain. Some reach volcanic soils, where water drains into the earth so fast and deep that few root systems can make any use of it. Others fall on the dark, acidic ground of spruce and fir forests. The same snowmelt that creates streamside gardens in one valley may liberate large amounts of gypsum and alkali, even selenium, in another, rendering thousands of acres brassy and chalk-colored, nearly bereft of life. There are chutes in the crotches of mountains where avalanches thunder down every few years, wiping out great huddles of young conifers; places where visitors can listen as ice pries loose slabs of granite, sending them crashing onto trees below.

Life in the Rockies is shaped both by spectacular forces—events like wildfire, heavy snowfalls, and howling wind shears—as well as by an array of far more subtle factors. North-facing slopes, out of reach of the drying fingers of the sun, give birth to lush forests as well as thick mats of forbs and wildflowers. High peaks snag moisture from east-bound clouds, in the process creating bone-dry rain shadows

on the other side. The simple fact of elevation can have profound biological effects. Mountain roadways plunge without
warning out of dark curtains of lodgepole onto sun-
drenched meadows of brome and sage. A traveler on foot
can be sulking in gloomy huddles of subalpine fir only to
thirty minutes later find herself on blinding runs of open
tundra. Elevation also influences the rhythms of animals.
Elk will in June nose their way to the high country barely
a few feet behind the receding snow line, nipping the
youngest, most nutritious plants; the first big slap of an
autumn storm sends them back again to the lowlands, to
winter range, where they paw through shallow blankets of
snow to reach the grasses below. It's elevation that created
the great agricultural conundrum of the West. As air rises, it
cools. And since cool air can't hold as much moisture as
warm, storm clouds driven up and over the mountains tend
to lose their cargoes at high elevations. In other words, the
very water that many agricultural crops need to survive ends
up delivered to places that are too cold for crops to grow.

Elevation creates incredibly dynamic plant communities—ones far quicker to react to changes in climate than
those found on more subtle landscapes, like those of the
Midwest or Great Plains. A person could walk all day across
a native swath of Nebraska prairie and only rarely leave a
basic weave of bluestem and Indian grass, grama and buffalo
grass. Not in the Rockies. Here groups of plants are knitted
closely together, separated by narrow mixing zones, called
ecotones. They respond fast to sustained drought or snow or

periods of heat or cold, either retreating down the mountain or advancing to higher locales. Which has proven a wonderful boon to climatologists and paleoecologists, who, by piecing together the tracks of those advances and retreats, have gleaned a much clearer understanding of how the North American climate has changed over the millennia.

Twenty thousand years ago the Rockies were an icebox. Splayed across the high mountains southward all the way to the San Juans of Colorado was a series of localized glaciers, many of them enormous, standing a mile or more thick. Yet from a climate standpoint these frozen expanses proved less important than still another reach of ice, located more than a thousand miles away—the Laurentide Ice Sheet, running out of eastern Canada toward New England roughly to Cape Cod. So significant was the Laurentide that it not only lowered temperatures across southern latitudes but shifted the jet stream far to the south. Storms that today routinely dump moisture on the northern Rockies for centuries saturated the southern Rockies, which were gaining forests while the northern range was losing them.

As the ice began melting, tremendous quantities of freshwater were loosed into the North Atlantic, raising the water level by more than three hundred feet. Freshwater released at various times by glacial Lake Agassiz alone, located in central Canada, was more than nine times the amount currently held by all the Great Lakes combined. Changes in temperature and salinity from the meltwater profoundly altered existing air and ocean circulation patterns; that in turn helped shift both the duration and depth of summer drought cycles. All of those events, and many more, left their mark in the folds of the Rockies.

There are lots of ways of unraveling such events, including the old favorite of counting tree rings, using thin slices of petrified wood; the wider the rings, the more favorable were conditions for growth. More useful still are the dark and gritty layer cakes of ancient sediment lying on the bottoms of Rocky Mountain ponds and lakes. From those bottoms researchers have taken core samples, typically eight or ten feet thick, making a kind of long-range calendar by determining exactly when the various strata were deposited. Because each layer contains millions of pollen grains and seed and leaf fossils, they serve as a good clue to the kinds of plants growing in the immediate area at a given time. Since scientists know the range of conditions in which each of those plants is capable of growing, they can make highly accurate estimates about the climate across thousands of years. In the same way, the absence of certain fossils in a given sediment layer—a lack of tree remnants, for example—might suggest that conditions were too cold to allow forests to survive. Likewise, such core samples contain layers of charcoal—evidence not just of fires per se but, more importantly, the conditions necessary for those burns to occur. Finally, there is typically in such material the presence of volcanic ash. In much of the northern Rockies, sediment cores show clear evidence of the massive Mount Mazama eruption 7,700 years ago in southwest Oregon, the event that gave birth to Crater Lake.

Studies at Colorado's Sky Pond reveal basic reactions to

changes in climate: timberline moves higher in warmer periods onto what before had been tundra, then is forced down again to lower elevations as temperatures begin to cool. Conifer forests in western Colorado were in the final centuries of the last glacial epoch as much as 2,000 feet lower than we find them today. Likewise, as the glaciers melted back, many of the highlands shifted from open parks and tundra to a thatchwork of temperate forest. In the north, lodgepole pine began the march to gain lands that had previously been occupied by Engelmann spruce and subalpine fir. Plants that for centuries were denied ground due to cold and ice wasted no time colonizing when the chance finally presented itself, moving quickly up the mountains, right behind the receding glaciers. (As useful as sediment layers can be, much of the Rocky Mountain West is too arid to support lakes, ponds, or other wetlands. In those places climatologists have managed to piece together the climate picture using pack rat middens found under rock overhangs and in caves, some of which contain the fossilized remains of plants gathered and stashed by rodents over thousands of years.)

As for what the future may hold, most computer models predict warming and drying across the Rockies, in part due to industrial pollution from greenhouse gases. This would lead not only to the demise of most remaining glaciers (since 1850 Rocky Mountain glaciers have shrunk by 30 to 70 percent) but to profound changes in the composition of plant communities. As moisture decreases wetlands will fade. Fire activity will increase. A recent study in Yellowstone National Park focusing on how trees might redistribute themselves in the face of anticipated climate changes predicts a major shuffling. According to this model, whitebark pine—a critical food source for the region's grizzly bears—will likely disappear entirely. The current mix, which has been in place for roughly 3,000 years, will be replaced by a blend of lodgepole pine and Douglas fir, along with newcomers like western larch, scrub oak, and ponderosa.

Curiously, the majority of our conservation efforts have long been focused on preserving plant communities that may not survive the coming climate change. Instead of worrying about maintaining these existing communities, some researchers say, it makes more sense to protect the widest array of habitats possible. Preserves with a range of elevations would allow plants to migrate upward in the coming world of increased warmth and drought.

OF COURSE there's the not-inconsequential matter of how these mountains got here in the first place. Many of the region's native cultures imagined the pieces falling into place in ways not unlike in the mythology of early Judaism: the world coming to life as the Creator let loose his breath on handfuls of earth. A devastating flood. Blackfeet tradition offers a classic earth-diver tale, the opening scene hung on an image of Old Man sitting high on a tiny island formed by a mountain peak, surrounded by floodwaters—beside him beaver, otter, duck, and muskrat. As powerful as Old Man is, he can't make the water recede, and in the end turns to the animals for help. What he needs to make dry land again, he explains, is the smallest amount of mud from the bottom of that ocean. Beaver goes first, only to drown in the attempt. The same for otter. Duck makes it back to the surface alive, but there's no mud in the webs of her feet. Then comes muskrat. She's gone for a very long time, and Old Man thinks her surely dead. But then she surfaces, unconscious, and on her paws is the tiniest dab of mud. Old Man carefully removes it from between her toes and blows on it, whereupon it grows bigger and bigger until it becomes all the land we see today.

Meanwhile Western civilization has had its own share of creation stories, most a lot less genial than notions of duck and muskrat swimming through the depths to recreate the world. In the thousand or so years from roughly 500 A.D. through the 1500s, Christian leaders routinely cast the high country of the world as an utter travesty, an affront to the state of perfection said to have existed shortly after the Creation, when the earth was round and smooth and sweet with order—when it was, as many clerics described it, a "mundane egg." Irregular landforms in general, and mountains in particular, were considered not part of the original creation but something that came later, a consequence of the Flood, put here by God as reminders of his extreme displeasure at our evil ways. Some religious scholars maintained that mountains were an upshot of Adam and Eve's fall from grace in the garden. Others insisted they were a literal curse on the earth, punishment on the soil for having soaked up the blood of Abel after he was murdered by his brother Cain. Throughout the era—long and deep and overflowing with bad dreams of wrath and punishment—there was no mistaking one of the central themes, a sordid twisting of an idea first offered by the Greek philosopher Lucretius, who had written in *De Rerum Natura* that the earth, like humans, was bound to become decrepit, decay, and die. By the time that notion got to Martin Luther some 1,600 years later, it had long been the bedrock of a religion that placed humans at the center of everything disagreeable. "Even the earth," wrote Luther, "is compelled to bear sin's curse."

Remarkable in all this is the quick dismissal of what had been a major tenet of early Christianity—namely, that with the coming of Christ not just humankind but the earth too had been redeemed. In that tradition nature wasn't something to be avoided but something to be embraced, a stage from which humans could unravel the lessons of the Creator. Yet this more holistic view—one that might have changed at least slightly the way countless generations treated the planet—was in the end crushed under the weight of some very different thinking. The revision gathered momentum under a growing fondness for an idea touted by the Roman philosopher Marcion, who along with some of the early Gnostics decided that Jesus wasn't in any way connected to the harsh, warmongering God of the Jews. If that was true, the logic went, then he also wasn't linked to the very earth that this more vengeful deity had created. The world of nature was irrelevant. Only later would the more familiar, more widely held belief arise which said spiritual purity depended on being able to overcome the corruptness of the physical world; all things of the earth, including the human body, were filled with one sort of horror or another—at best a prison for the soul, at worst a home for the devil.

As late as the seventeenth century leading poets, philosophers, and religious leaders of the Western world routinely described unkempt landscapes in degrading terms, referring to mountains as tumors, blisters, pimples, carbuncles, and warts. There were a few quiet exceptions. Benedictine abbess Hildegard von Bingen spoke in the twelfth century of *veriditas,* the "greenness" of the creative power of God, manifesting itself through every corner of creation. "The soul is in the body the way the sap is in the tree," she writes, "nourishing and sustaining the body instead of struggling against it." The early Kabbalist Jews living in Iran were thinking similar thoughts, offering how God is like a tree upside down, with the roots in heaven and the sap running to earth and bringing spiritual energy to all the world. Even the Green Man, a common archetype in the pagan societies of northern Europe, consisting of human faces with vegetation growing out of them, thus denoting our oneness with nature, shows up in a surprising number of nooks and crannies of Christianity. Green Man remains a resident of nearly every Gothic cathedral in Europe and Great Britain—hovering over the doorway of the church of St. Michel d'Aiguilhe, across the portals at Chartres, scattered about Exeter. So too does he wait at the base of the magnificent cathedral tower of the Freiburg in Breisgau, where directly below, in the nave of the minister, other Green Men grieve over the fallen Christ. Yet as impressive as all this might be, such sensibilities were in the end no match for official distaste for the earth and flesh. The same vegetation that poured out of the mouth and nose of Green Man would during the Catholic Reformation come to be identified with sexual sin. Not by accident does much of European art of the period portray Adam and Eve with their genitals covered by leaves.

Despite the sheer level of anxiety most Westerners felt about rugged landscapes, such feelings would ease dramatically in the seventeenth century, when there was an explosion of curiosity about so-called irregular landforms. Some historians postulate that the spell was broken by the influence of other cultures. Art from the Far East, for example, was finding its way into Europe with increasing regularity, most of it presenting nature in general as a place of spiritual rejuvenation. Such a perspective may well have influenced Western poets and artists, many of whom began linking their own poetical notions of the earth to emerging fields of science. The invention of the telescope, for example, along with the resulting discovery of various astral bodies, created in some a tremendous sense of possibility, a "psychology of infinity," as poet and philosopher Henry More put it. Furthermore, many considered Galileo's discovery of mountains on the moon proof that such landforms were less a consequence of sin than simply a benign act of creation. (Why would a symbol meant to steer the masses, after all, be placed where so few could see it?) The Creator was a dramatist, Henry More wrote time and again, a master author who packed his "Tragick Comedy" with unimaginable levels of mystery, beauty, and variety. At the same time, however, many Western scientists and religious leaders despised the Eastern spiritual tenet of respecting nature. As scientist Robert Boyle put it, such attitudes proved "a discouraging impediment to the empire of man over inferior creatures." Firmly on Boyle's side were men like Descartes, who declared nonhuman life to be nothing more than complex machinery, incapable of reasoning, speech, and, by some readings, even sensation.

Still, poetry and science would continue to mix, turning into a kind of gentleman's game where privileged fans of art also began pursuing studies in astronomy, biology, and physics. At least for a little while, such disciplines were only occasionally at odds with the teachings of the Christian church. Indeed, for a time the Book of Genesis seemed to have enough holes and vagaries in it to allow God to grow at a rate roughly equal to the expansion of knowledge. (It's worth noting that in earlier Judaic and Islamic traditions science had never been about cobbling together a rational understanding of the world, but rather was an exercise for the imagination, something to help practitioners overcome ordinary states of consciousness.) This easy relationship between the church and science came to a screeching halt later in the 1600s, in large part thanks to the emerging science of geology. While those staring into microscopes and telescopes could be seen as simply adding texture to the biblical creation story, geology—and in particular the fossil records it revealed—was from the beginning on a collision course with heresy, its first offense being to turn on its head the 6,000-year time span the church had long said God needed to create the world.

One man battered by church wrath was Thomas Burnet, an amateur naturalist and theologian whose entire life would be pushed, pulled, and at various times nearly destroyed by mountains. In 1681 he completed the first edition of *The Sacred Theory of the Earth: Containing an Account of the Original of the Earth, and of All the General Changes Which It Hath Already Undergone, or Is to Undergo, till the Consummation of All Things.* Added to throughout his life, the work eventually consisted of *Two First Books Concerning the Deluge, and Concerning Paradise, and Two Last Books Concerning the Burning of the World, and Concerning the New Heavens and the New Earth.* Burnet never really meant to be controversial. Indeed, he originally set out to head off the growing struggle between religion and science, maintaining that science was nothing more or less than a new set of revelations about the divine. Unlike most other writers, though, Burnet made his case in dramatic, stirring prose, lending a palpable sense of dread to his images of the world crumbling in the face of flood and fire. He speaks of the sun heating waters inside the earth and causing them to burst forth in great eruptions, reaching enormous heights. "And then rowling back again, [the water] would sweep down with it whatsoever it rusht upon, Woods, Buildings, living Creatures, and carry them all headlong into the great gulf. Sometimes a mass of water would be quite struck off and separate from the rest, and tost through the Air like a flying River; but the common motion of the waves was to climb up the hills, or inclin'd fragments, and then return into the valleys and deeps again, with a perpetual fluctuation going and coming, ascending and descending, till the violence of them being spent by degrees, they settled at last in the places allotted for them; where bounds are set that they cannot pass over, that they return not again to cover the Earth." From a purely literary perspective he was a master, compared often with Plato and Milton. The sheer force of his writing left tracks in the work of some of the greatest poets of the Western world, from Coleridge to Wordsworth.

Literary merits aside, in the years following the publication of *Sacred Theory* Burnet was accused of being something close to an agent of the devil. To begin with, he'd had the gall to suggest that the world evolved not by the intervention of God per se, but rather by natural scientific principles the Creator set in motion long before. In one of the original Genesis stories, for example, the Bible speaks of waters being divided from the waters. Burnet happily explains this as the result of the heaviest parts of the seas sinking downward to form the interior parts of the earth. Likewise, "that which swims above would also be divided by the same Principle of Gravity into two Orders of Bodies, the one liquid like Water, the other volatile like Air." Just as oil floats on water, so too would "a fat, soft, and light Earth spread across the face of the oceans." Far from considering himself a heretic, Burnet figured he was doing precisely what early religious leaders had intended, learning to read clues from the earth—this time through science—thereby coming to better understand the genius of God.

Burnet's perspective was often disturbed, however, by existing irregularities of the land—in particular, mountains. To look upon the highlands, he said on several occasions, was to gaze on "a world lying in its rubbish." Like his contemporaries he was at various times convinced that such landscapes were a result of the Great Flood, which created "wild, vast and indigested Heaps of Stone and Earth—ruins of a broken world." But whereas other scholars saw the Flood as a specific act of divine wrath, Burnet carried on with his central theme, considering it a process built into the earth from the very beginning. In the center of the earth, he explained, was a central fire, capped by a watery membrane—sort of like an egg white enveloping a yolk. This in turn was wrapped in an ovoid shell, extended slightly toward the poles. The weight of massive amounts of rain falling from the skies, along with the fiery touch of the sun, caused a crack in the frame of the earth, thereby releasing the waters hidden underneath. This in turn led to all the aforemen-

tioned screeching and general upheaval, and ultimately to
those dark and twisted mountainscapes we see today.

If theologians were quick to denounce Burnet as a
heretic, so too were many learned men eager to tackle him
on scientific matters. It was in this splendid outburst of
opinion—in particular, reactions to Burnet's theory of
mountains—that we find the foundations of modern geology. Some leading minds of the day claimed the high country rose from a process of fermentation, like so much bread
dough (or beer, as Isaac Newton suggested). From still other
scientists came the ever popular sudden shock theory,
whereupon the uplands rose by a sudden explosion of something in the earth akin to wildfire or gunpowder. One com-
mentator—a soon-to-be-famous astronomer by the name of
Halley—agreed with Burnet's comments about the ability of
the Deluge to afflict the world, making mountains where
there were none before, but suggested the real cause of that
flood was the striking of the earth by a mighty comet. At the
very least, as author Marjorie Hope Nicolson points out,
whether you agreed with him or not, Burnet's work had the
striking effect of making his fellow Englishmen conscious of
mountains to an extent never known before.

Some scholars suggest it was a trip to the Alps that led
Burnet to begin weaving his *Sacred Theory* in the first place.
Oddly, while that mighty reach of high country often
repelled him, in other moments it thrilled him to the point
of obsession. "Suppose a Man was carried asleep out of a
plain Country amongst the Alps," he writes, "and left there

upon the Top of one of the highest mountains, when he wak'd and look'd about him, he would think himself in an inchanted Country, or carried into another world. . . . Rocks standing naked round about him; and the hollow valleys gaping under him. . . . He would hear the Thunder come from below, and see the black Clouds hanging beneath him; upon such a prospect it would not be easy to persuade himself that he was still upon the same Earth." (This fondness for imagining the high country as otherworldly has formed the backbone of most of the world's mountain lore. An almost identical reaction to Burnet's rose 150 years later among travelers crossing the Rockies on the Oregon Trail. "A person to be placed [at South Pass] of a sudden," wrote W. W. Chapman in 1849, "would wake in their dream that he had escaped from this earth, would think he was in realms unknown.")

The greatest "Objects of Nature," Burnet went on to say, just pages before once again trashing the highlands, are the most pleasing to behold. "And next to the Great Concave of the Heavens, and those boundless Regions where the Stars inhabit, there is nothing that I look upon with more Pleasure than the wide Sea and the Mountains of the Earth. There is something august and stately in the air of these things that inspires the Mind with great Thought and Passions." What's important to note is that Burnet wasn't responding to some new flash of rational understanding, but rather "to the pleasure found in an imagination that expanded in the presence of wild, vast and undigested nature." The design was marvelous, so much so "that it ought rather to be consider'd as a particular Effect of the Divine Art than as a work of Nature." As unremarkable as those statements might seem today, they were in truth the tip of an iceberg of aesthetic change in the Western world, stretching the definition of beauty beyond what most would've thought possible.

There would be others, including staunch critics of Burnet, who in the end made their own contributions to changing the way people looked at mountains. From the church side came Richard Bentley, preaching that it was unreasonable to assume that a figure in nature with a regular shape was any more beautiful than an irregular one. "All bodies are beautiful that are fit for their proper uses and ends. We ought not then to believe that the mountains are misshapen because they are not exact pyramids or cones." But for Bentley, as well as for noted scientists like Edmund Halley and John Ray, the real argument that mountains were proof not of a curse but of divine wisdom was the growing understanding of the high country as a primary driver of the hydrological cycle. Mountain springs, pointed out Halley, were the chief sources of rivers like the Danube, the Rhine, and the Rhône. "It may almost pass for a Rule that the magnitude of a River . . . is proportionable to the length and height of the Ridges from whence its Fountains arise."

Naturalist John Ray, meanwhile, one of the most learned botanists of the seventeenth century, encouraged people to try to see the sharper aspects of nature not as a curse but as proof of genius in their design. The thorns of the rose, he pointed out, were but a clever protection against grazing animals. Mountains were deserving of respect both as the birthplace of rivers as well as for their spiritual inspiration, their tendency to encourage "higher thoughts" in the beholder. With the idea of a biblical curse on the earth fading, a celebration of irregular landscapes blossomed in the work of philosophers. By the early 1700s men like the Earl of Shaftesbury were seeing magnificence even in the most barren regions of the world; while even vast deserts may in a sense be ghastly, he noted, such places weren't without a peculiar beauty. The earl, like many who came later, was increasingly inclined to compare the relationship between God and nature to that between the artist and his art. Nature had intrinsic value. It was about more than just serving the whims of humans.

Thirty years after the publication of *Sacred Theory* mountains would no longer be repelling travelers on their famous Grand Tour, but enticing them. By early in the eighteenth century the same rugged, unforgiving uplands that harbored minions of the devil, feared by even the most fearless knights, were being considered by some as the source of godly wisdom, a reality check on vanity, a clue to the path for those with the courage to move past the easy, spineless life of the formal garden.

Burnet is sometimes referred to by historians as one of the fathers of English Deism, a precursor to that brand of reason-based faith held by many of the founding fathers, including Thomas Jefferson and Benjamin Franklin. (There is a Creator, say the Deists, revealed through individual effort and discipline, but he's not up there fine-tuning our lives.) Yet every bit as significant was Burnet's stirring if somewhat shaky affinity for the wild—a bond that would still be bearing fruit just as Americans were going from colony to nation, forever changing the way we came to think about the land sprawling from our back doors. Contrary to the claims of some authors, Americans did not embrace wild places only at the point their technology allowed control over them. Of far greater consequence—for them, as well as for most other peoples of the world—were shifts in attitude about what such places were said to reveal about the divine.

AS FOR THE ROCKY MOUNTAIN CREATION STORY offered by modern science, what it lacks in divinity it makes up for in complexity and astonishment. To most people the geology of the Rockies is a train wreck. Hearing someone describe it over the course of a long afternoon can create the kind of mind warp that first hits us as kids, spinning ourselves dizzy trying to imagine how it's possible to go a zillion miles into space and not be an inch closer to the end. Yet thanks to exposed fossils lying about in certain Rocky Mountain strata—everything from brachiopods to bivalves, coral to crinoids—it's possible at fortunate moments to envision the region as nothing but layers of sand and mud in the gloom of an ancient sea.

Fired deep within the earth, the first draft of the range—the so-called ancestral Rockies—rumbled and groaned over millions of years in slow, magnificent upwellings, punched and buckled along drifting faults, finally reaching elevations more than three miles high. The range was then worn down by erosion, rock after rock splitting and washing downslope, until the landscape was nothing but a flat plain again. More recent times brought other uplifts, including the Laramide orogeny of roughly 60 million years ago, creating the basic structure of the mountains we know today. Along the way came an astonishing 30-million-year run of volcanic activity, spewing ash by the millions of tons. In one location alone, near the present town of Silverton, Colorado, is a mound of volcanic debris from that restless period measuring more than forty miles across and three thousand feet deep. Later, hot water coursing through cracks and along quartz veins embedded in the rock deposited the gold and silver that would one day bring miners by the thousands.

For all this rock and rumba and belching of earth, the force most obvious to the average visitor—that aspect of geology that has so much to do with our immediate impressions of the range—is ice. Visible within the upper tucks of the summits are large, graceful streaks of snow. Some are remnants from 20,000 years ago, when winter came in heavy blankets, the snow falling in quantities well beyond what could melt in a single mountain summer. Becoming thicker year by year, they turned into glaciers, ultimately reaching depths more than five times the height of the Empire State Building. In time gravity began nudging them downward, inch by inch, causing them to move with such force that they not only widened valleys but polished the sides of entire mountains, wrenching cliffs and knife-edged arêtes out of solid granite, picking up house-sized boulders from high peaks and dropping them in the middle of low valleys and plateaus, cutting basins into abrupt cirques with blue lakes and hanging waterfalls nearly too beautiful for words.

Climbing today onto the highest reaches of the alpine tundra, there's no missing the webs of fissures and hairline cracks spread across the boulders, slowly widening as water continues to freeze and expand in the joints. It's a process that goes on all year, even in summer, breaking truck-sized boulders into modest loaves, then fist-sized rocks, then scree, and finally into the sand that washes down and out onto the plains some 6,000 feet below. On this same tundra can be found odd circles of rock, highly symmetrical polygons squeezed out of the earth by freeze and thaw. On patches of bare soil are glassy strands of needle ice—three-to-five-inch-long spikes pointing down into the earth, drawing moisture from the soil and at the same time lifting dirt to the surface, where it will blow away on summer winds. The same inch of soil that at this elevation took a thousand years to make can be peeled away in a single afternoon.

Wrapping these patches of needle ice are thick mats of tundra, exquisite weaves of sedges and grasses and arctic willow, tufted hair grass and pussytoes and wildflowers by the dozen—in places a near carbon copy of what's found twelve hundred miles to the north, on the windswept hummocks of the Arctic. Exactly where trees end and tundra begins in the Rockies depends on where you happen to be. In general the tree line rises at a rate of about 300 feet for every degree of latitude traveled; all things being equal, a conifer that manages to struggle to the 12,000-foot mark in New Mexico would in southern Montana make it only to 9,000 feet. Only on the ragged edges of the tundra do we find the last stalwart champions of the trees—whitebark pine in the northern reaches of the range, limber pine in the central and north-central Rockies, bristlecone pine in the south. Most have been beaten to their knees by wind and ice, growing old as much by growing out as up. Krummholz, some call it. Crooked wood. Or as it was known for a long time in Colorado, wind timber. To say that growth comes slow to such trees is a colossal understatement. A bristlecone pine above Santa Fe, New Mexico, barely five inches across, standing no higher than a man of modest stature, may well have sprouted about the time of the Roman gladiators.

The real world of trees begins lower down, underneath these more rugged survivors. Dark huddles of Engelmann spruce and subalpine fir. Magnificent ponderosa pine, low and scattered in the north, higher and more dense to the south. There are the enchanting, highly aromatic pinyon-juniper groves of northern New Mexico and southern Colorado—and near them, Gambel and Emory and silverleaf oak, standing side by side with buckbrush and sumac and mountain mahogany. These latter species aside, it's no accident that a trip across the slopes of the Rockies is more often than not a trip through evergreens. Rather than wasting the first slice of an all-too-brief growing season putting on leaves, spruce, fir, and pine are through their needles able to conduct photosynthesis any time of the year. Just as important, the conical shape of conifers—especially pronounced in high-elevation species like subalpine fir—allows them to shed snow loads that would easily crack and slough the branches of deciduous trees. The notable exception is the aspen, a tree of truly Catholic tastes, found at elevations ranging between 5,000 and 10,000 feet. Cut off from the explosion of colors that spray across the hardwoods of the East and the Midwest, residents of the Rockies will often raise their arms to a mountainside covered in aspen and assure you that what the region lacks in color, it more than makes up for in grace.

Aspen is the most widespread tree on the North American continent; in the Rocky Mountains it makes up a scant 1 percent of the total forest, and yet wherever it appears it is beautiful enough to break your heart, bringing unexpected whimsy to this world of timber and stone. In older groves the smooth bark wears the freehand scratches of a thousand travelers long gone—claw marks from grizzly and black bears, initials carved in the trunks by Mormon sheepherders during the first half of the twentieth century. In the same way a thirsty man might look down from the mountains for a sign of cottonwoods, which only grow near water, trappers in the early 1800s turned their eyes upward from the valleys and scanned for aspen, knowing they were among the favorite foods of beaver. In modern times it's been used for pulpwood, but during much of history aspen was largely spared by lumbermen. A few groves were taken here and there for corral posts, mine timbers, and furniture, even shredded as packing material for fruits and vegetables. A few more were harvested during the nineteenth century, carved into kitchen utensils for pioneer wives.

The leaves of the aspen are forever in motion, rustling, a flutter on the mountainsides not unlike the sound of a fast-stepping stream. The great French traders of the north—the *coureurs du bois,* the "runners of the woods"—said the rustle was actually a tremble, and that it started the instant aspen was chosen as the wood for the cross of Christ. A lesser-known tale from Germany says that one day the Holy Family was out walking in a forest and all the trees bowed—all except the proud aspen, that is, which led Christ to curse it, setting all the leaves to shaking. Native tales of the tree, on the other hand, are entirely different—less tragic than astonishing. Like the Ute story, which says the colors the aspen wears in autumn are the result of the day Great Bear smelled the hunter's cooking fire. Drawn in by his hunger, Great Bear approached and a fracas ensued, a full-blown fiasco, and when all was said and done yellow cooking grease and red blood were spattered all across the leaves of the forest.

That a deciduous tree like the aspen could thrive in the harsh folds of the Rockies has a lot to do with the fact that most new growth comes not so much by means of seed as by root extensions, or suckers. Following a devastating fire or avalanche, these suckers blast out of the earth like so many jack-in-the-boxes, needing only a couple of years to cover the ground with young trees. In the wake of an old patriarch falling over will come hundreds of shoots, each young tree providing a succulent feast for moose and deer. A single burned acre may within two years bristle with the shoots of thousands of trees. It's an efficient system. One aspen forest south of Utah's Wasatch Mountains has been touted as the largest living organism on the planet: covering roughly 120 acres, the grove sports over forty-seven thousand individual trunks, with an estimated total biomass of more than thirteen million pounds.

To anyone who wanders the Rockies, be it in the cool of the woods or on great patches of blooming tundra, there will come the sense that this is a young country. Millions of tons of rock lie about in chunks, still to be turned to soil. Thousands of streams have yet to punch clear pathways to the valleys below. Even old, established systems are tenuous. Mature runs of spruce-fir forest on the north side of a mountain may, with nothing more than a flick of lightning, be reduced in hours to a smoldering ruin, 300 years from full repair. While countless writers have told of feeling diminished in the Rockies, a greater impression still is the one brought on by life and death forever crashing and blooming in these chutes and meadows and timberlands. A sense of beginning, of life fresh out of creation.

CHAPTER 2

The Rise of the Mountain Man

***The Trapper's Bride* (1847)**

ALFRED JACOB MILLER

Fur traders routinely took Indian wives, despite a fierce prejudice against such practices by many Americans. This ceremony is being conducted at the camp of the bride's people, as was the usual custom.

WHEN THOMAS JEFFERSON FIRST ACQUIRED the area west of the Mississippi through the Louisiana Purchase in the spring of 1803—spending the grand sum of $15 million to double the size of the United States—there was no shortage of critics. Some, like Delaware senator James White, decried the move on economic grounds. Others worried the acquisition would lead to the formation of a new confederacy. More common than either of those was the feeling that, as Henry Adams put it, such swashbuckling acts of empire-building "made blank paper of the constitution." A reasonable point, considering the Constitution contained no provision for acquiring land by means of treaty.

As it happened, in the years following the acquisition there came great demand for beaver felt hats among gentlemen throughout Europe; some Americans were quick to grasp not only that there was economic value to exploiting the furs of the Far West, but, more important still, that the presence of trappers in the region might be a good way to lay claim to important trading opportunities on the Pacific, many of which were under British control. Businessmen like William and Henry Ashley set up major fur companies that either bought pelts from free trappers or, more often, turned trappers into company men, providing them with the equipment and support they needed to exist in the wilderness. Not that this was a new idea. British, French, and even American trappers had by then been roaming the streams and rivers of the continent for decades. The heyday of trapping in the Rockies, though, can be said to have started when the following newspaper ad appeared in the (St. Louis) *Missouri Republican* on March 10, 1822:

> To enterprising young men: The subscriber wishes to engage one hundred young men to ascend the Missouri River to its source, there to be employed for one or two or three years.

While pop culture has long been fond of painting the mountain men as crude and unrefined, this was no simple gang of hooligans. With the exception of Anglo women, trapping appealed to a remarkably diverse population, including a number of black Americans. In fact, as the trapping era progressed, in some regions of the Rockies it became increasingly common for blacks to be among the only traders trusted by the natives. Some, like Edward Rose and James Beckwourth—men who back in the states were thought of by some as less than human—rose to extraordinary status among the Indians. Rose not only spent time actually living with the Crow, often dressing in the finest native clothing, but had tremendous influence over much of what happened across some seven thousand square miles. He was treasured by the children of the tribe, who ran to meet him with great shouts, arms outstretched to the sky. Then there was Moses Harris, known regionally as "Black Harris," born a slave in either Kentucky or South Carolina, gaining his freedom as a young man to head west in 1823. Moses earned great distinction as a mountain man, and was known far and wide for his ability to endure brutal privations. General William Ashley expressed the greatest confidence in his knowledge of the country surrounding the upper Missouri and Yellowstone Rivers. As the fur trade weakened, Harris went on to help locate and build Fort Laramie, and was later highly sought after as a scout for westbound missionaries on the Oregon Trail. Moses left Oregon Territory in 1847 for St. Louis, Missouri (a state in which slavery was legal), where he died just two years later, of typhoid. His epitaph reads:

> HERE LIES THE BONES OF OLD BLACK HARRIS
> WHO OFTEN TRAVELED BEYOND THE FAR WEST
> AND FOR THE FREEDOM OF EQUAL RIGHTS,
> HE CROSSED THE SNOWY MOUNTAIN HEIGHTS
> WAS A FREE AND EASY KIND OF SOUL,
> ESPECIALLY WITH A BELLY FULL.

It took both intelligence and resolve to pull off life as a trapper, and those unwilling to learn the skills necessary for dealing with both the wilds and its native occupants fared badly. Some estimates indicate that at least one in five trappers lost their lives within the first year on the trail. On occasion the odds were even worse. Out of 116 trappers who left Santa Fe in the spring of 1826, only 16 survived to the following spring. That said, some of the most comprehensive research to date suggests that well over half of mountain men died of old age, the average life span being sixty-four—slightly better than the average longevity of adult males in the country as a whole. Barely one in ten perished at the hands of Indians.

The profession also required startling levels of endurance. As historian Francis Parkman put it, "I defy the annals of chivalry to furnish the record of a life more wild and perilous than that of a Rocky Mountain trapper." Consider a couple of days like those described in the journals of trapper James Clyman. In February of 1824 Clyman, along with friend and fellow trapper William Sublette, were moving up the Popo Agie River near Wyoming's Wind River Range. After a long, fruitless search in the cold for game, in the last of the twilight the pair spotted three bull buffalo in an open run of sage; given that the horses were too weak to give chase, the men crawled over the crusted snow with guns held in the crooks of their arms, hoping against hope for the chance at a decent shot. With his fingers nearly frozen Sublette pulled the trigger, and by a combination of skill and miracle the bullet found its mark. Growing more numb by the minute, clumsy with hypothermia, the men scoured the ground for a few handfuls of dry sage, built a fire to lay the meat on, and a short time later watched helplessly as a brutal north wind reared up and scattered the flames, pelting their faces with sand and snow.

At this point Clyman and Sublette called it quits on cooking dinner, deciding to get some shut-eye. Instead they spent a brutal night tossing and turning on the hard, frozen earth. When daybreak finally came Clyman crawled out from under his buffalo robe to launch a desperate search for more scraps of firewood, telling Sublette to remain in bed and keep his fingers warm, nimble enough to strike a fire. Clyman managed to get the firewood all right, but in the few seconds it took Sublette to pull his hands out from under the robe and position the flint and steel above the tinder his fingers started to freeze, making the work impossible. And with that the heroic William Sublette—the man who once shot a grizzly off Jedediah Smith's head, the intrepid guide who would six years later lead the first wagon train across South Pass—wrapped his buffalo robe around his shoulders and prepared to die, refusing all Clyman's urgings to saddle up and ride. Determined not to abandon his friend, Clyman tried several more times to kindle a flame. No luck. Finally, in a last desperate act, he ran his hands through the ashes of the previous night's short-lived fire, where he found a single coal roughly the size of a corn kernel. This he placed in a nest of shredded bark, then leaned in close and blew it into a blaze. "My friend got out and crawled up to my side, and drawing our robe around our backs we tried to warm ourselves but the wind being so strong the smoke and fire came into our faces."

By now it was abundantly clear to both men that their only hope was to get out of the wind; Clyman packed up the meat and saddled the horses, intending to make for a dense patch of timber several miles away. After placing Sublette on the lead horse, he took up a position immediately behind, urging and prodding, quickly realizing that sitting on horseback, not moving his body, was a sure way to freeze to death.

He dismounted again and began a long plod through the snow. "I saw my friend was too numb to walk so I took the lead for the last half mile and struck a grove of timber where there was an old Indian lodge but one side of which was still standing." Setting a quick fire, Clyman eased his friend off his horse and led him to the blaze. "He seemed to have no life to move as usual; he laid down nearly asleep while I went broiling meat on a stick. After a while I roused him up and gave him his breakfast," at which point Sublette "came to and was as active as usual. I have been thus particular in describing one night near the summit of the Rocky Mountains, although a number similar may and often do occur."

The following evening, Clyman and Sublette, having rejoined other members of their party, watched as a violent wind rose out of the north, leaving the pair awake all night clutching their robes to keep them from flying away. In the morning they used their blankets to fashion a screen for the fire, but once again the back currents of a ferocious wind filled their faces with smoke and ash. Having had quite enough, they removed the windscreen, at which point the fire blew away across the prairie. The remainder of the next two days was spent lying under clumps of willow wrapped in their blankets, "it being the only way to keep from perishing the blast being so strong and cold."

If cold and snow wasn't knocking, there was always the challenge of dealing with unfriendly tribes. In Blackfeet country John Colter, formerly of the Lewis and Clark expedition, routinely set his traps at night, gathering up the har-

vest at dawn and then hiding out the rest of the day. Pad-
dling one morning on a small stream near the upper Missouri in 1808, he and partner John Potts—also of the Lewis
and Clark team—found themselves suddenly surrounded by
Blackfeet warriors, motioning them to shore. Having no
choice, they paddled over, at which point an angry brave
wrested the rifle from Potts. Colter managed to yank it back
from the Indian and hand it to his partner, who got off a
shot, killing one of the braves. He was immediately cut
down by a volley of arrows, and Colter knew his own death
was imminent. Furthermore, he understood enough of the
language to know the chief was discussing the most entertaining way of dispatching him. Several of the warriors
opted for tying him to a tree and using him for target practice, but that didn't seem sporting enough to the chief, who
suddenly asked Colter if he was a fast runner. While in truth
Colter was an outstanding athlete, he assured the chief he
wasn't, at which point the decision was made to strip him
naked and set him loose across the prairie—a region peppered with prickly pear cactus, mind you—in a rousing game
of hunt-the-human. After a couple of miles Colter had left
all but the strongest runners behind, then turned around and
killed his closest pursuer with his own spear, stole his blanket, and ran to the Jefferson River, where he hid nose-deep
in cold water under a raft of driftwood. The angry braves
searched for hours, but came up empty-handed. At which
point Colter wrapped himself in the blanket, gathered a few
roots to eat, and began a two-hundred-mile, eleven-day

barefoot walk to Fort Raymond. Colter would have several other encounters with the Blackfeet, and it was likely that fact as much as any other that finally sent him back to Missouri, where he built a cabin, married a woman named Nancy Hooker, and had a son. By 1813 he was dead—victim not of spears or arrows or bears, but jaundice.

How mountain men dealt with these on-the-job hazards suggests a kind of toughness for which today there are few equivalents. Thomas "Pegleg" Smith, who left home at sixteen to escape beatings from both his father and his schoolmaster, while working as a mountain man had his leg shattered by an Indian bullet. Using a butcher knife, he amputated the limb himself, then turned the blade on a pine log, carving a wooden leg that could be quickly removed for use as a club. Which was a good idea, given Smith's fondness for brawling, stealing horses, and taking up with some spirited Indian women, at one point amassing five wives from various tribes of the central Rockies. (One of these wives was killed by another in the throes of a jealous rage; Smith claimed to have buried her along the shore of Bear Lake in northeast Utah, a place she was especially fond of, in a standing position so she could overlook the lake.)

A typical trapper with a lone packhorse carried a half dozen steel traps, each weighing about five pounds, as well as a powder horn and bullet pouch, tobacco sack and pipe, a small wooden box containing beaver bait, a butchering knife and fire-making implements—and for some, a hatchet fastened to the pommel of the saddle. Each beaver trap was connected to a three-to-five-foot long chain, on one end a swivel ring. Setting the trap meant wading out into the shallow part of a stream not far from the bank and digging out a bed to rest it on, eight or ten inches under the water, and then covering it with mud. The end with the ring was played out into deeper water, out near the center of the stream, then anchored to the bottom by a length of dry willow branch called a float. Finally, the tip of another willow branch was dipped into the bait—a substance called castorum, taken from glands at the base of the beaver's tail—then shoved into the mud with the baited tip hanging above the jaws of the trap. (Though castorum had long been used by Indians of the Northeast, mountain men turned the practice into a fine art, spicing the bait with everything from nutmeg to cloves to alcohol, fiercely guarding the recipe. In St. Louis at the height of the fur trade, such potions fetched ten to twelve dollars a bottle.) On catching scent of the castorum a beaver would come to investigate; standing on his hind legs under the tip of the baited branch, he sprung the trap. Unable to reach the bank—those that did often chewed off a foot to escape—the animal was eventually swung into deep water and drowned. Once harvested, it was immediately skinned and the pelt allowed to dry; this was then folded in half with the fur facing to the inside, forming a light bundle easily carried by a packhorse.

For their part, beaver weren't exactly dim-witted rodents, there for the taking. The animals learned fast from the sudden demise of their kin, sometimes remaining trap-shy for months. Some claim it was for that reason, every bit as much as for preserving breeding populations, that many trappers were reluctant to harvest more than a few animals from a single family group. Those who tried outsmarting beaver by switching the usual location of their traps—placing them, for example, in well-traveled runways—reported seeing animals swimming around them, even using sticks to spring the jaws. (Then again, trappers did have superior imaginations.) In the end, though, the mountain men had the upper hand. By the late 1830s, as hat fashions in Europe were shifting fast to silk, Rocky Mountain beaver were well on their way to being trapped into oblivion. When Europeans first arrived in the New World there had been perhaps 400 million beaver on the continent, stretching from the Arctic to the Rio Grande. Two centuries later, just over 2 percent of that number remained.

We know a lot about the daily life of the Rocky Mountain trapper because so many—some historians figure at least one in five—left histories in their own hand. In his fine work *The Mountain Men: A Statistical Review*, researcher Richard Fehrman suggests that at least a third of trappers were literate, while other scholars estimate that rate to be much higher, barely below the literacy rate in America as a whole. Most were at least bilingual, and some were also well tutored in Greek and Latin. Writing in *Life in the Rocky Mountains* about a stay in the northern Rockies, Warren Ferris gives a clear sense of the need for being skilled at language. "Our little village numbers twenty-two men, nine

women and twenty children; and a different language is spoken in every lodge, the women being of different nations,
and the children invariably learn their mother's tongue
before any other. There were ten distinct dialects spoken in
our camp, each of which was the native idiom of one or
more of us, though French was the language predominate
among the men, and Flathead among the women."

Writing to his brother from the northern Rockies in
the summer of 1826, Daniel Potts offers remarkable detail
about the location of rivers, forage, wildlife, climate—even
scenic attractions. Underneath it all is a deep sense of satisfaction with his surroundings. A large valley in present-day
Wyoming he describes as being "adorned with many flowers
and interspersed with many useful herbs . . . the most beautiful scene of nature I have ever seen." From this location,
Potts tells his brother, he crossed the Wind River Range,
where "I unfortunately froze my feet and was unable to
travel from the loss of two toes." That memory in turn leads
him to share his enormous admiration for "the humanity of
the natives (the Indians) towards me, who conducted me to
their village, into the lodge of their Chief, who regularly
twice a day divested himself of all his clothing except his
breech clout, and dressed my wounds, until I left them." As
so many others would do in the decades to come, Potts concludes his letter by telling his brother that just weeks ago he
was on the verge of returning home—and yet, "owing to this
unexplored country, which I have a great curiosity to see, I
have concluded to remain one or two years."

Not that the musings of mountain men were limited to daily events. When he wasn't wrapped in blankets shivering for his life with his friend Sublette, James Clyman liked to ponder such confounding issues as the speed of light. Rufus Sage, meanwhile, busied himself for years comparing the Sioux tongue with Latin, proposing that at some point the Romans had shown up on this continent and handed off their language to the natives. His notes offer a long stream of comparisons between Latin words and their Sioux counterparts, at the same time outlining in painstaking detail similarities in sentence structure. The Latin word *appello,* Sage explains—meaning to declare or proclaim—is also present in the Sioux language, and carries the exact same meaning. *Cogor,* in Latin being one who collects or brings together, compels, forces, or heaps up, in Sioux refers to a maker of things, a manufacturer, one who produces by arranging materials. *Tepor,* warmth in Latin, he contends is the root of tepee in Sioux.

Pater, pronounced alike in both languages, in Latin implies father, but in Sioux means fire. Sage explains the discrepancy by pointing out that the Sioux consider the great ball of fire in the sky to be the father of all things. "The relationship disclosed between these two languages," he concludes, "is seemingly too close and significant to be attributed to mere chance or accident. In former ages the Romans maintained a foothold upon the American continent, and had intercourse with this nation, either by arms or by commerce."

These sorts of quirky rambles, along with a constant sharing of stories from favorite books by literate trappers, were common fodder around winter camp. Osborne Russell, one of nine farm children born in Bowdoinham, Maine, and the man who penned the highly literate *Journal of a Trapper,* dubbed such gatherings the Rocky Mountain College. "I doubt not but some of my comrades who considered themselves Classical scholars," he writes, "have had some little added to their wisdom in these assemblies, however rude they might appear." Even uneducated mountain men sometimes left winter camp a little wiser. The legendary teller of tall tales Joe Meek was taught how to read over the course of one winter by a fellow trapper named Green. By early spring he was perusing copies of the Bible, as well as a tattered collection of Shakespeare someone had toted into camp.

Nor did the learning stop when the trapping era ended. Osborne Russell settled on the Snake River at Fort Hall and devoured books on geology, chemistry, and philosophy. Shortly after moving west to the Willamette Valley in Oregon Territory, he lost his right eye in a blasting accident. During convalescence he turned again to books, this time studying law—a bout of do-it-yourself scholarship that led in 1843 to Russell's appointment to the Supreme Court by the executive committee of the provisional government of Oregon. Likewise, the freshly literate Joe Meek would head west from the Rockies at the close of the trapping era to become part of the Oregon provisional legislature. In time he would consort with President James Polk in an effort to secure formal territorial status for Oregon; when that happened in 1848, Polk appointed Meek as the first federal marshal of the territory.

IN ADDITION TO men like Russell and Meek, both of whom had pulled themselves up by their bootstraps, there was another trapper common to the Rockies—the kind of man destined to become a social phenomenon in these mountains right into modern times. These were the sons of well-off American, English, and European families, the black sheep of mothers and fathers who no doubt prayed their offspring would get over their itch for wilderness and come home to be decent boys, which when it happened at all tended to take far longer than most parents thought reasonable. As the celebrated black trapper Jim Beckwourth observed about his peers, Indians had a much harder time learning to live like white men than white men did becoming like Indians.

A case in point is Antoine Reynal Jr., son of a prominent French family that settled in St. Louis around 1776. Reynal took to the wilds at an early age, working at various times as a trapper, trader, stage operator, and all-around vagabond. Like a number of his contemporaries, he poured himself into the world of the natives with abandon—marrying a Sioux woman, routinely traveling with the tribe in traditional garb, even hunting game with Sioux weapons. As a result he sometimes took snide hits from men of privilege and power traveling the West, incensed that someone with such a background would turn his back on the fineries of civilization to take up with people considered by many to be scoundrels and savages.

The great historian Francis Parkman, who crossed paths with Reynal at Fort Laramie in 1846, wasted no time dismissing him as nothing but a sleek and selfish vagrant, living in a "wretched oven-shaped structure made of begrimed and tattered buffalo hides stretched over a frame of poles." It was a strange comment from a man who claimed to have spent most of his life driven by a fierce love of the wilderness and those who lived there, who years later would mourn the fact that civilization had led to the destruction of the Indian and frontiersman, "a class of men so remarkable both in their virtues and their faults, that few will see their extinction without regret." By the 1870s Parkman was altogether despondent about the trapper having vanished—men not unlike Reynal—their lives nothing more than a distant memory. Yet in truth it was only from a distance that the famed historian was able to embrace those things that went against the grain of his upbringing as a proper Bostonian.

As it turned out, Parkman wasn't the only man of reputation to cross paths with Reynal. In the summer of 1860 the old trapper was managing a stage stop near Laramie, Wyoming Territory, his fortunes waning at the hand of tribes increasingly hostile to whites, when who should show up at his door but the famous explorer Richard Burton. Never one to shy away from xenophobic commentary, Burton was more impressed with the old trapper than with his trappings—in particular, his wife—"the usual squaw, a wrinkled old dame," whom he quickly dismissed as another one of those hardworking but sorely ill-favored beings. Burton did for a time find himself smitten with Reynal's beautiful half-breed daughter, though in the end he managed to rise above his feelings, declaring that people of mixed blood belonged "to a sub-species that has diverged widely enough from the Indo-European type to cause degeneracy, physical as well as moral, and often, too, sterility in the offspring. Half-breeds are like the mulatto, quasi-mules. The mongrels are short-lived, peculiarly subject to infectious diseases, untrustworthy, and disposed to every villainy." To be fair, Burton didn't invent this churlish attitude. Some of the most respected scientists in America had been spouting those same views for well over a decade. And Burton was known to backpedal now and then, at one point freely acknowledging that "some of the noblest men in the land are descended from 'Indian princesses.' "

While politicians, scientists, and church leaders spoke strongly against mixed-blood marriages and the offspring they produced, in truth there was a profusion of such families, up and down the Rockies and across the plains. Sacagawea, the wife of Frenchman Toussaint Charbonneau, had served as a liaison between the men of the Lewis and Clark expedition and various native groups, including her own native Shoshone people. She traveled with her infant son, Baptiste, and the presence of the pair went a long way toward conveying to other tribes that this was not a warring party. (The only serious scrape the Corps of Discovery had with the natives was on their return trip from the Pacific—a skirmish with the Pigeon for which Sacagawea wasn't present.) The men took no small inspiration from her resilience. Likewise Alexander Culbertson, who as the boss, or "booshway," of Fort Union, near the confluence of the Missouri and Yellowstone, was easily the most important capitalist on the upper Missouri, married a member of the Blackfeet named Medicine Snake Woman. It was she who helped Governor Isaac Stevens achieve his Pacific Railway Survey in 1853 and, nine years later, educated Lewis Henry Morgan, the so-called father of American anthropology, about the complex kinship systems of the Gros Ventre and Blackfeet cultures. Edwin Thompson Denig, who became widely recognized as the world's foremost authority on the Assiniboine, would've been hard pressed to earn that reputation without the help of his Indian wife, Deer-Little-Woman.

Furthermore, though the children of such marriages were often subjected to cruel prejudice, they were hardly the slackers Burton and the scientists made them out to be. Sacagawea's son Baptiste was at various times a mountain man in the Rockies, a gold miner, and a justice of the peace in California. While still a youth he traveled extensively in Europe, adding to the existing list of Indian languages he spoke a fluency in Spanish, French, and Italian. As historian John Ewers points out, Baptiste could discuss with equal fluency "French philosophy, Spanish dances, the trapping of beaver, or the uses of Indian medicine bundles."

After spending hours with Reynal at the stage stop listening to his stories of having left home at an early age, of several marriages, of being a captive of the Pawnees, Richard Burton concluded that there were two kinds of men in the Rockies, one good and one bad, and that Reynal was of the better sort. Here was the true mountaineer, often from an honored and wealthy family, yet driven to the wilds by the ills of society to become "the forlorn hope in the march of civilization." The second type of Rocky Mountain man, on the other hand, Burton dismissed as the refuse of the eastern cities, men "compelled by want, fatuity, or crime to exile himself from all he most loves." Leaning hard on his Victorian sensibilities, Burton explains that good guys like Reynal invariably passed through a preliminary stage of greenhorn to become a man in every sense of the term—going beyond Indian bravery and fortitude to unite "the softness of woman and a child-like simplicity, which is the very essence of a chivalrous character." You could read his nature in his clear blue eyes, Burton says, his suntanned countenance, merry smile, and frank and fearless manner. "By climate and its consequences, by that huge magnificence of nature and the violent contrasts of scenery, the [man of the Rockies] takes on a remarkable resemblance to the wild Indian." And with that Burton tossed more wood onto the flames of that favorite mythical motif of every Englishmen, as well as a great many Americans of the day—that of the reclusive woodsman, being tested and found pure of heart.

Burton was especially intrigued by how many of the old mountain men he ran across were accomplished story-tellers—transcendental liars, he called them—products of imaginations inflamed by scenery and danger. "I have heard of a man riding eighty miles, forty into camp and forty out, in order to enjoy the sweet delights of a lie. His yarns and stories about the land he lives in have become a proverbial ridicule. He has seen mountains of diamonds and gold nuggets scattered like rocks over the surface of our general mother." Burton shares a handful of those tales, including one that serves as a reminder of how often men of the wilderness stripped biblical themes down to something closer to their pagan origins. "I have been gravely told," he writes, "of a herd of bison which arrested the course of the Platte River, causing its waters, like those of the Red Sea, to stand up, wall fashion, while the animals were crossing." Curiously, when three Montana travelers by the names of Cook, Peterson, and Folsom returned from the upper Yellowstone country in 1869, having weathered extreme dangers in the shadows of the Blackfeet, Cook ignored all encouragement to turn their adventures into a magazine article. There's little doubt, he explained, that any such account would be dismissed as "the too vivid imagination of a typical Rocky Mountain liar."

Such storytelling seemed for mountain men a clever

game, the object being to weave startling images about a land that on most days was too outrageous for language itself. Thus trapper Jim Bridger finds himself in the bizarre, spectacular world of Yellowstone, making good use, he explains, of a certain massive canyon where he can toss off a loud yell right before bed, only to have the echo come back around again in time to rouse him from slumber the next morning. He walks through petrified forests, where not only the trees have been turned to stone, but also the animals, grasses, even birds in flight. On crossing Alum Creek, which takes its name from a highly astringent sulfate present in the water, Bridger discovers that all the animals have on drinking it shrunk to a fraction of their original size.

Yet another character who would've ranked high on Burton's list of good mountain men was John Moncravie, born in Bordeaux, France, at the end of the eighteenth century—a young man of privilege who turned his back on society to answer the call of adventure in the Rockies. When he was a young boy Moncravie's family left the motherland to settle in Philadelphia, where he stayed until enlisting in the army in 1820. Moncravie was a compact, spirited fellow with enormous artistic ability. John James Audubon met him at Fort Union in 1843, and the two men became fast friends. Audubon grew ever more impressed—not just with Moncravie's remarkable fishing, hunting, and boatmanship, but also with his inspired acting and comedic impressions, which he happily unfurled at the slightest encouragement. Moncravie was a cheeky sort, as when in 1856 he negotiated with the Sioux tribe for a forty-nine-square-mile parcel of land, to be ceded to him personally, negotiating with the Indians as legally only the government could do.

LIKE MOST CHILDREN OF REFINED PARENTS who chose the path of a trapper, Moncravie would never have passed muster in polite Philadelphia society. On a single trip up the Missouri River, traveling on keelboats full of goods bound for the Blackfeet, he threw a party for himself and fellow boatmen by tapping into four hundred dollars' worth of his boss's whiskey. During his lifetime Moncravie took several Indian wives, losing the first one rather quickly at Fort Union when, as recorded in the notes of a friend, "one Joseph Dechamp seduced from the Bed and board of Doctor McCrevee [*sic*] his own lawfully purchased wife which he obtained from her father for the sum of $280 in merchandise."

It's fascinating to think of the fineries someone like Moncravie would have been exposed to as a young man, considering that as a trapper he probably didn't own even a change of clothes. The vast majority of mountain men wiped knives and hands covered with blood, grease, or beaver castor onto their buckskins until the leather was no longer gold, but a shiny black. For some, crude habits were hard to break. When in 1895 the burgeoning city of Denver decided to launch the first Festival of Mountain and Plain, legendary trapper Jim Baker—often touted as Colorado's first white citizen—along with former trapper John Albert were invited to serve as marshals. Having proudly rolled out the red carpet for these dignitaries by booking them rooms in a fine hotel, the festival committee was appalled to learn that Baker not only refused to take a bath—"I already had one this year"—but spurned the toilet in favor of the alley behind the hotel.

Hygienic gaffes aside, more surprising still is that so many of these men, born into families with high regard for bloodlines and social position, routinely burned their familial bridges to the ground. When Moncravie died at age eighty-eight he made no mention of having any relatives at all, distributing part of his modest estate to the Masons, some to a local church, and the remainder to a woman in Brownville, Nebraska, named Abigail Shadley. Again, much of the anger leveled at trappers from their families of origin had to do not so much with their footloose lifestyle as with what seemed a dreadful willingness to embrace Indian culture. Granted, by the time men like Moncravie hit the wilds most people had rejected the Puritan view that said any frontiersman who cavorted with Indians was a traitor to his race. Yet any willingness to give Indians the benefit of the doubt crumbled at the thought of having one for a relative.

AS THE NINETEENTH CENTURY WORE ON, increasing numbers of Americans were pulled to the Rockies by a fiery notion of untold riches in the gold fields of the high country. For the most part, mountain men didn't bite. When the good times for trappers ended around 1840, relatively few proved willing to hunker down later over a gold pan in some two-bit mining camp in the Sierras, let alone start farms or become merchants selling harnesses and bolts of cotton to the newcomers. It was not a situation suited for sober calculation, wrote trapper Zenas Leonard at the end of the fur trade era. Some mountain men, he noted, were altogether careless about what would become of them, wanting to turn in with and live the life of the Indians. Two or three others were anxious to leave the wilderness and return to the states. "But this," Leonard says, "was rejected by nearly all." These were men who'd participated in what historian Richard Slotkin considers a main theme of early America, the shredding of conventional European mythology in order to get back to a more primary source of "blood knowledge" of the wilderness. And there was no place that shredded conventional myth faster than the Rockies. It was a land beautiful and dangerous and at times startlingly unpredictable, and for many the thought of leaving—or, nearly as bad, living there en masse, bound by routine—was simply unbearable.

This reluctance to leave the Rockies, sometimes after being out of touch with civilization for years, was from the very beginning a common theme. Englishman John Bradbury of the Liverpool Philosophical Society was traveling up the Missouri in 1810 when his party spotted three men in two canoes descending the river along the opposite shore. Bradbury's party fired their rifles to signal the men, who paddled over to exchange greetings. "We found them to be three men belonging to Kentucky," Bradbury writes, "whose names were Robinson, Hauberk, and Reesoner. They had been several years hunting on and beyond the Rocky Mountains, until they imagined they were tired of the hunting life; and having families and good plantations in Kentucky, were returning to them. But on seeing us, families, plantations, and all vanished. They agreed to join us, and turned their canoes adrift."

When in 1806 the Lewis and Clark expedition was at last homeward bound, having been in the wilds of the West for some two years, on an August day at the Mandan villages in present-day North Dakota they happened upon two trappers from Illinois, heading for the Rockies. Anxious for advice from the famous Corps of Discovery, the trappers took a chance and encouraged John Colter—a fine and trustworthy woodsman, as well as an excellent hunter—to drop his plans to return to St. Louis and instead come along with them to the upper headwaters of the Missouri. Colter didn't blink. He requested and received a discharge from the Corps of Discovery, turned on his heels, and headed back upstream into the wilderness, where he worked as a trapper for several years. Colter eventually pried himself away years later only with difficulty. "Now if God will only forgive me this time and let me off," he reportedly told Thomas James, "I *will* leave the country day after to-morrow—and be damned if I ever come into it again."

Still another member of the Lewis and Clark expedition, George Drouillard, was back in the mountains shortly after returning to St. Louis, though he died a few years later at the hands of the Shawnee. Almost a half century later one Sam Curtis, of modest means, penned a letter to a friend advising him to pack his bags and head for Colorado the following spring. "If you do not make much out here you will find a new kind of life and an entirely new character of people and country. For my own part I am not going back to the States to live for five years at least. I do not say I will stay here, but with a rifle and a pony I can go anywhere between this and the Pacific."

Now and then even more official types had trouble leaving. Reporting on one of Ferdinand Hayden's expeditions to the Rockies in 1878, the *New York Times* shared an unflattering rumor being circulated in the West that Hayden was running in circles. "In proof of these charges, says the *Times*, it is stated [by western newspapers] with charming directness, that Prof. Hayden has been guilty of surveying the same 'hitherto unknown fields' year after year, and of 'discovering' the same highest mountain half a dozen times."

CHAPTER 3

A Faith Moved by Mountains

Long Jakes, The Rocky Mountain Man (1844)

CHARLES DEAS

To people living near the frontier, mountain men were simply hard-working small businessmen. For much of the rest of the country they were, as New York art critic Henry William Herbert described this painting, a celebration of the "glorious, the free, the untrammeled sense of individual will and independent power."

A HALF CENTURY AFTER THE AMERICAN Revolution, with the fur trapping era in full swing, there remained among the population a spectacular impression about the wild—namely, that it was a perfect antidote to the hated aristocracies of Europe and England. Nature as the great equalizer. Out in the boondocks, after all, privilege counted for nothing. It mattered not a whit who your daddy was, the level of blueness in your blood, how much money was stuffed into your mattress. Wilderness made "obsolete and alien," as conservationist Peggy Wayburn describes it, "the old ideas of rank, caste, and inherited aristocracy." Clearly the old English habit of seeing nature as a model of class society—common people were "trashy weeds or nettles," as Timothy Nourse said in 1700—didn't ring true in a culture where people spent much of their time in the shadows of the wilds.

With the economic panic of 1819, grave concerns began to arise about whether capitalism—in particular, the way it seemed to be leading to an unintended concentration of wealth—would one day swallow up this promise of equality. To dream of the Rockies was for many easterners not just a longing for peace and quiet (that would come later) but a dream of independence—one that showed itself first through images of trappers, then scouts, and finally cowboys. Such characters were appealing not for reasons of glamour, but because they seemed to be in control of their fate at a time when the average man felt his own measure of control slipping away.

Stories about mountain men changed dramatically the farther you got from the frontier. In 1830s St. Louis, trappers were typically regarded as small businessmen, clever and adaptable, doing a dangerous job but enjoying a considerable amount of freedom out in the wilds. Among the people of New York, meanwhile, it was the freedom and swashbuckling elements that got noticed, brightened over time and finally amplified to mythical levels. Writing mid-century in *New York Illustrated Magazine,* critic Henry William Herbert was beside himself with praise for a Charles Deas painting of a mountain man called "Long Jakes," first displayed in New York in 1844. The man in the portrait, he assures his readers, is nothing less than a celebration of the "glorious, the free, the untrammeled sense of individual will and independent power."

Never mind that trappers were in truth almost never loners, nor fiercely independent. Because much of their work was conducted in hostile territory, most were part of brigades of from twenty to forty men; some trapped, others guarded horses, and still others skinned and took care of the pelts. Such groups often held their equipment in common, and whatever was taken in the way of furs ended up being equally divided among all. Winter camps were even more communal, with the days spent hunting, repairing equipment, telling stories, holding shooting competitions. The majority of mountain men were married, many had kids, and a significant percentage traveled with their families by their side.

At the same time eastern art critics and other sophisticates were savoring the nobility of the trapper's freedom, mountain men were the focus of similar themes in books. Fictional stories of Rocky Mountain trappers mark a dramatic shift toward an American hero more wild and reckless than any who'd come before—especially when compared to that previous star of the frontier, James Fenimore Cooper's Leatherstocking. (In *The Prairie* Cooper attempted to catch the western wave by sending Leatherstocking to the Rockies to become a trapper. Sadly, our hero was clearly out of his element. As D. H. Lawrence pointed out, Cooper loved the wildness of his hero, but at the same time seemed afraid he might belch at dinner.) The fictional mountain man was among the first American characters to be shaped not so much by the act of preparing wilderness for civilization, as Daniel Boone had done, as by a full-blown retreat to the wilds. What writers and readers alike noticed most was the degree to which he'd taken on Indian ways; whether that was a good thing depended entirely on who was telling the story.

In the early years of writing about mountain men most of the favorable press went to Rocky Mountain trapper Kit Carson. As it happened, Kit was the favorite guide of the enormously popular explorer John Fremont; even better, his image was routinely made ready for the page by Fremont's wife, Jesse, a highly skilled editor. In other words, Carson had a public relations agent working for him, one careful to portray him in terms friendly even to religious conservatives. This wasn't some rude thug from the mountains, but one of those spirit-filled Leatherstocking types, a man who'd gone into a wilderness filled with beasts and sinners and all manner of other temptations, and by force of character and grace of God came out unsullied. The lengths writers went to in order to sanitize Carson were ludicrous. Forced to discuss a hell-raising spree the trapper had gone on in Santa Fe at the end of an expedition in 1831, biographer De Witt Peters nearly chokes on political correctness. "Young Kit, at this period of his life, imitated the example set by his elders, for he wished to be considered by them as an equal and a friend. He, however, passed through this terrible ordeal, which most frequently ruins its votary, and eventually came out brighter, clearer and more noble for the conscience-polish which he received. And contracted no bad habits, but learned the usefulness and happiness of resisting temptation, and became so well schooled that he was able, by the caution and advice of wisdom, founded on experience, to prevent many a promising and skillful hand from grasping ruin in the same vortex." (Carson himself is said to have later cringed at this description, complaining that Peters had "laid it on a little too thick.")

This "deliverance by nature" theme was with Carson, as it had been with other heroes of the frontier, further proof that by the mid 1800s the virtues of the wild—at the very least, as an agent of transformation—had seeped into nearly every corner of the culture. Writing in 1873 about Carson in Yellowstone, historian John Abbott talks of his refined appreciation for the wonders of nature—a perfect fit with his native delicacy of mind. A delicacy so refined, Abbott tells us, that it never allowed him to use a profane word or to take a sip of alcohol (neither of which is true), or for that matter to be guilty of any impure action at all. Carson was just a simple man who loved to mingle his own spirit with "the silence, the solitude, the grandeur with which God has invested the illimitable wilderness."

Meanwhile, in conservative circles mountain men without the Carson-style public relations team didn't fair so well, at least not until later in the century. This was in part due to the fact that just as the Rocky Mountain fur trade was hitting its glory days, a rather different movement was burning across much of the United States, particularly in the South and Midwest. Championed by religious leaders as "the second great awakening," this was Christian revivalism at its most brazen—and a large part of what moved writers like Alexis de Tocqueville to conclude that Christianity had taken center stage in the New World. What makes comments like that of Tocqueville so notable was that, Puritans aside, America wasn't known as being especially keen on organized religion. It's been estimated that in much of the country roughly 40 to 50 percent of the population weren't members of any specific church; even in religion-prone New England, that figure was close to 30 percent. As John Burroughs would later write, "If we do not go to church as much as did our fathers, we go to the woods much more."

One of the major appeals of the second great awakening was that it offered to reclaim Christianity from the growing influence of a colorless, utterly rational kind of secular thinking. There was a strong populist feel to the movement, which proved a refreshing change from the slurry of guilt that had long been pouring from the Calvinist traditions. Not that the second great awakening didn't have plenty of hellfire. But now the individual, unassisted by preacher or priest, was again deemed capable of building a relationship with the Creator—not by producing particular works, but by making whatever sacrifices were necessary to get in touch with the power of the Holy Spirit. It was a theology well suited to a frontier nation—a promise to protect a person's spiritual path from both the tyranny of wealth and the antiquated ritual and ceremony that seemed to plague the religions of Europe.

The Protestants found their leader in one Charles Finney, born in Warren, Connecticut, in 1792. Young Charles was only a small boy when his parents moved to the brush and tumble of western New York. Like many of their neighbors, the Finneys weren't a religious family. In his youth Charles heard but a few sermons, most of those from the occasional "ignorant preacher" wandering the countryside—men who offered such drivel that Finney's clearest memories were of people gathering after prayer meetings to laugh at their ignorance. Then, in the autumn of 1821, while enrolled as a law student in Adams, New York, Finney drew what was the most hungered-for blessing any Christian of the day could hope for. He had a revelation. On his knees, in the woods, in the leaves and the brambles.

Finney's revival-based ministry, as full of brimstone as the calderas of Yellowstone, would within a year of its inception claim more than a hundred thousand supporters. Before long, revival meetings were sprouting up across much of the country, thick with wail and swoon. Ministers were housed and fed in the homes of their followers, their every waking minute spent either at the church conducting the actual revival or eating and drinking with large groups of mostly women, the entire swarm bent on splendid conversation, and of course saving as many souls as the good Lord would allow. Not everyone was impressed. Certainly not Englishwoman Frances Trollope, traveling through the Midwest in 1831 conducting research for her book *Domestic Manners of the Americans*. After having for miles heard locals beside themselves with excitement about this or that revival, during a visit to Cincinnati she finally got the chance to see one in person—as it happened, of the Presbyterian variety. Judging by her notes, she was in any given moment either thoroughly bemused or utterly horrified.

Well-mannered Presbyterian or Methodist ladies, she explained, were forever angling against one another to have one popular preacher or another be the star of their revival, much the way a blue-blooded lady of England relished landing a fashionable poet. But it was the theatrics of the revival meeting itself that put her on edge. She describes the gnashing, sweat-soaked delivery of the revival preacher, intent on making his flock come to weep in horror before the fires of hell. "And as Rebecca made known to Ivanhoe what she saw through the window, so the preacher made known to us what he saw in the pit that seemed to open before him. The device was certainly a happy one for giving effect to his description of hell. No image that fire, flame, brimstone, molten lead, or red-hot pincers could supply—with flesh, nerves, and sinews quivering under them—was omitted. His eyes rolled, his lips were covered with foam, and every feature had the deep expression of horror it would have borne, had he, in truth, been gazing at the scene he described."

A curious aspect of these revivals was the considerable sexual tension they produced. Writing about camp meetings in Shelby County, Tennessee, author J. M. Keating talks about how easy it was in such emotionally charged settings for the mind to become bewildered and confused, passions careening out of control. Which is no doubt why "for a mile around camp the woods seem to be alive with people; every tree or bush had its group or couple, while hundreds of others in pairs were seen prowling around in search of some cozy spot." No surprise that months later came tittering rounds of gossip about so-called camp meeting babies. One family doctor advised the evangelists to close up shop, since by all appearances they seemed to be making souls faster than they were saving them.

Even Mrs. Trollope was taken aback by what she considered open displays of sexuality, including one woman she spotted in the throes of religious ecstasy, her "chin and bosom wet with slaver." Still, in the end Trollope concluded that such commotion was simply a means for American women to amuse themselves. After all, she conceded, they could hardly go to the theater. Nor were they allowed to play cards. By all appearances they were working awfully hard for their families, and for that reason alone they probably deserved some sort of relaxation. "For myself," she writes, "I confess that I think the coarsest comedy ever written would be a less detestable exhibition for the eyes of youth and innocence than such a scene."

It was in large part this religious fervor that led churches to launch missionary drives to save the souls of Indians in the Rockies and Far West. There'd been talk of such outings in the past, but by and large little backing from the churches. How is it, Samuel Parker had wondered, that an adventurous man wanting to traffic commercially in the wilds of the West could put together an amply funded team while the Christian heart, stirred also to head west, "would plead in vein for two thousand dollars and less than a handful of men." Over time, strengthened by the flow of more and more politicians making the claim that subduing western lands was a part of God's plan, the pleas of religious leaders like Parker started getting results; by the 1840s a growing stream of missionaries from all faiths were making for the mountains. Most seemed inclined to unleash their faith in the Rockies with the same threats, the same brittle promises of hell and damnation that had marked the first great awakening in New England a hundred years earlier. There was one road to salvation, they made clear, and it was a route of great personal sacrifice and pain. And while that message would mirror beautifully the manifest destiny diatribes being bandied about by men set on conquering the West, the Indians found it less than compelling. As a result, early missionaries were routinely snubbed for their low conversion rates.

Mountain men didn't help the batting average. Most were little inclined to moral improvement—or so the novels written about them at this time would seem to suggest. Uptight New England author Timothy Flint unveiled a new work called *The Shoshonee Valley*—one of the earliest pieces of fiction about the Rocky Mountain West, and among the first to cast mountain men as primary characters. Flint pulls no punches laying out the unsavory aspects of such a life in the wilds, one aimed only at satisfying man's most base impulses, with its dangerous joys of "unrestricted love and licensed polygamy." Novelist Charles Sealsfield concurred, filling his readers' heads with the idea that the real trapper of the Rockies "hates mankind and kills any rival with fiendish joy."

Ironically, the only way the faithful could reach the missionary field was to employ as guides the very heathen mountain men who were such a terrible threat to Christian values in the first place. Trappers hired to lead preacher Jason Lee westward proved a constant irritation. "We might have a congregation of some hundreds to preach to today," he lamented one Sunday along the Oregon Trail, "yet we have no doubt that were we to propose such a thing it would be rejected with disdain and perhaps with abuse, for all hands nearly are employed trading, drinking or some such amusement. My God, my God, is there nothing that will have any effect upon them?"

Preacher Samuel Parker seconded Lee's frustrations, struggling to minister to a group of trappers at rendezvous near Jackson Hole in 1835. Mountain man Joe Meek confesses that it was a wild and motley congregation, not so given to piety as sarcasm and mocking levity. Halfway through the sermon a herd of buffalo was spotted near the end of the valley, at which point "every man made haste after his horse, gun, and rope, leaving Mr. Parker to discourse to vacant ground." Two years later preacher William Gray noted how there was in fact no Sabbath in this country, that it was a region of desolation and profanity, where the mountain had cast off all fears of both God and man.

Asa Smith laments that while several men had listened to his sermon on July 1 titled "God Is Love," some even listening with apparent attention, "there is little hope of benefiting them." Cushing Eells, meanwhile, describes a dance by Indians and mountain men outside his tent as the emissaries of Satan worshiping their own master. How was it, he asks in his diary, that white men brought up in a civilized land can appear to so much imitate the devil? Then again, "it is said that many of the white men in the mountains try to act as much like Indians as they can and would be glad if they really were so." Of those religious conversions that did happen among mountain men, many were short-lived. Trapper James Connor confessed his faith and was baptized in

1839; within four years he'd been kicked out of the church for the sins of Sabbath-breaking, fighting, selling liquor, neglect of religious duties, and polygamy.

If the missionaries found the mountain men disagreeable, the mountain men were often less than thrilled with the preachers. Marcus Whitman, among the earliest to head west, in a masterful piece of understatement writes to the church board about his experiences with an American Fur Company caravan: "Very evident tokens gave us to understand that our company was not agreeable, such as the throwing of rotten eggs at me." In time feelings softened toward Whitman, both for his kindness as well as because his years as a country doctor allowed him to help stop what could have been a deadly outbreak of cholera. But for others the walls were up, and they would stay up for decades to come. Writing in the *Atlantic* in 1898, Rollin Lynde Hartt says the average Montana businessman "objects to walking on the same side of the street with a church. There is still more truth than fiction in the old saying that 'west of Bismarck there is no Sunday, and west of Miles City no God.'" This condition Hartt blames on church leadership, which he says has long been using the Rockies as a "ministerial ash heap and dumping ground" on which they gladly fling their outcast clergy—"vicious men, disgraced men, renegades of all shades and colors."

Despite the shortcomings of the humans in the Rockies, the mountains themselves were to many religious leaders never anything less than thrilling. On first spying the peaks from a distance, their summits clad with snow, Jason Lee declared them "most grand, beautiful, and sublime." Writing from Devil's Gate, of all places, the Reverend Edwards Parrish describes the scene as "quite romantic, with rocks, mountains and plains, the sun with its native majesty beautifying the whole. O, my soul, read in nature, nature's God." John Wood tells of the same scene as having "a great display of God's works," while Theodore Talbot declares it "a place to contemplate the wondrous ways of the Deity."

THE LIVES OF THE MOUNTAIN MEN shone a light on a long-standing paradox of the Rockies, providing all the necessary ingredients to make a case either for or against a life in the wilderness. Strong men like Kit Carson were presented as if they were the next best thing to Jesus Christ—out there drifting through the dark folds of the high country, resisting all temptations. Others saw the trapper as a full-blown heathen, his life a slap in the face to everything sacred. (Curiously, the two reactions suggest the faint tracks of a pair of opposing mythologies common in ancient times: one associated the very direction of the West with renewal and freedom, while the other cast it as the province of death, darkness, and passion.) Muddying the waters still more, art critics and various other intelligentsia on the Atlantic seaboard were thrilling to notions of the Rocky Mountain trapper as the symbol of freedom, an important hedge against the growing influence of corporate wealth.

One of the most famous paintings of the nineteenth century, Thomas Cole's *The Oxbow* is a narrative of wilderness being transformed into more human-centered landscapes. (Courtesy The Metropolitan Museum of Art, Gift of Mrs. Russell Sage, 1908. (08.228) Photograph © 1995 The Metropolitan Museum of Art)

This painting by Albert Bierstadt was completed in 1863 and exhibited to great acclaim. By the end of the century, Bierstadt was being criticized for relying too much on imagination. The artist responded that he placed "no value on literal transcripts from nature." (Courtesy The Metropolitan Museum of Art, Rogers Fund, 1907. (07.123) Photograph © 1979 The Metropolitan Museum of Art)

Thomas Crawford's mammoth work, which adorns the Senate Pediment on the East Front of the U.S. Capitol, was a comment not just on the nature of progress but also on the cost of that progress to both native culture and landscapes. (Architect of the Capitol)

Henry Farny, who was as comfortable in the company of frontier ruffians as with the nobility, proved a master at capturing the dramatic backdrops of the Rocky Mountains.

Despite the imposing nature of Fort Laramie (a private fur trading station), Alfred Jacob Miller's renderings of both the interior and exterior of the place suggest a certain camaraderie between white traders and the Native Americans. (The Beinecke Rare Book and Manuscript Library, Yale University Library)

Boom times came to sleepy Leadville, Colorado, in 1877, on the heels of a rich silver strike at Fryer Hill. By 1879 nearly fifteen thousand people had crowded in, served by more than fifty grocery stores and some one hundred twenty saloons. (Courtesy Colorado Historical Society, CHS.X4784, George D. Wakely)

Popular images of lone men panning for gold suggest less about the nature of mining, which by the 1860s was fast on its way to becoming a thoroughly industrial affair, than they did about a fierce dream Americans had to be footloose in the wild Rockies. (Courtesy Denver Public Library, Western History Collection, Louis Charles McClure, MCC-1918A)

No corner of the Colorado gold rush proved more challenging than the San Juan Mountains. The terrain was rugged, railroads were slow in coming, and there were limited supplies of gold. Ute Indians violently objected to interlopers in what they considered vital hunting grounds. (Courtesy Walker Art Studio, Center of Southwest Studies, Fort Lewis College, Collection P042)

Out of roughly 35,000 cowboys working cattle in the American South and West, historians estimate that between five and ten thousand were black. (Courtesy Denver Public Library, Western History Collection, X-21563)

The dude ranches of the Rockies introduced women to the three cornerstones of Western recreation: horseback riding, hunting, and that most uniquely enduring of outdoor pursuits—fly fishing. (Courtesy Denver Public Library, Western History Collection, Z-3100)

The Valley Ranch
HORSEBACK TRIP
IN THE ROCKIES
for Young Ladies

Yellowstone National Park
Wyoming Big Game Country

JULY—AUGUST

BRAND

Brownie Newton

A 1924 brochure from Wyoming's Valley Ranch. "Lately the dude ranch has taken its place in the social calendar as a thing that one must do," reported the *New York Times*. (Buffalo Bill Historical Center, Cody, Wyoming; MS14.2C.1/3)

There would be no ultimate truth in the Rockies, no single vision shared by either the trappers or those watching from a distance. Yet between the two extremes of infatuation and fear was no end of possibilities. In the same way the jumbled mountainscape of the Alps had left Thomas Burnet soaring on "the pleasure found in an imagination that expanded in the presence of wild, vast and indigested nature," the Rockies were expanding the minds of a great many Americans. As the twentieth century was dawning, Rollin Lynde Hartt would write that Montana was "everything, by turns or all at once . . . incoherently American—a national vaudeville, a social kaleidoscope, an incongruous complex of the innumerable, irreconcilable, incompatible elements that make up the nation."

In the decades to come there would be plenty more to raise the eyebrows of proper easterners—continued consorting with the natives, a pervasive mocking of organized religion, an early and surprisingly steadfast push for woman's suffrage. In a sense the Rockies were like the two grizzly cubs Zebulon Pike brought back from the mountains of Colorado as a gift to Thomas Jefferson. Not sure what to do with such odd souvenirs, Jefferson passed them on to his friend naturalist Charles Wilson Peale, who was horrified when the animals began terrorizing his family. In the end the unlucky little bruins were shot, stuffed, and mounted in a museum.

CHAPTER

Slow and Restless, Revengeful and Fond of War

Westward the Course of Empire Takes Its Way (1861)

EMANUEL GOTTLIEB LEUTZE

No idea in American history was more vigorously sold than the notion that God himself was calling us to the Pacific. As the wilderness fell, however, many found the hunger for empire turning into national melancholy and regret.

WHILE MANY TRAPPERS FOUND THE Indians of the Rocky Mountains much to their liking, plenty of others did not. The first known Europeans to roam the range were a group of Spaniards in 1540, led through the foothills of New Mexico's Sangre de Cristo Range by Francisco Vásquez Coronado. Like many explorers who would follow, Coronado was obsessed with legends of gold. In truth such stories had long been favorites of the Spaniards, beginning with the tale of the Seven Cities of Antilla—a fantasy ignited during the Moorish invasion of Spain, when seven Portuguese bishops were said to have packed up their congregations and sailed west, eventually stumbling across seven golden cities on an island somewhere in the Atlantic. Likewise a similar legend—the Seven Cities of Cibola—promised fabulous wealth near a cluster of native settlements at Zuni Pueblo, in present-day New Mexico. Coronado wasted no time investigating.

Such frantic searches typically involved terrorizing the natives. At Pecos Pueblo one of Coronado's men, Hernando de Alvarado, pressed into service a Plains Indian captive known only as the Turk, who promised to take the soldiers not to Cibola, but to another land of riches called Quivira. Week after week Turk led Alvarado northeastward onto the plains into what is now Kansas, on one of the great wild-goose chases of a land that would one day be known for wild-goose chases. It was only a matter of time before the Spaniards realized they'd been had, intentionally drawn away from the native villages by this charlatan, this Turk. At which point they strangled him to death in an iron garrotte. By September of 1541 the Spaniards were crossing back over Glorietta Pass, swearing to hunt for riches another day.

Change was slow to come. A hundred and fifty years later bishop of Chiapas Don Bartholomew de las Casas wrote a book-length manuscript to King Charles V chronicling a firsthand view of the incredible abuse of native populations by the Spanish government on other New World lands farther to the east. Bartholomew called his work *An Account of the First Voyages and Discoveries Made by the Spaniards in America . . . Containing the most exact relation hitherto published of their unparallel'd Cruelties on the Indians, in the destruction of above Forty Millions of People.* It is among the most disturbing accounts of torture ever laid down, with graphic descriptions—most of them supported by woodcuts—of everything from roasting natives on spits to cutting babies from the womb. "They laid Wagers with one another, who should cleave a Man down with his sword most dexterously at one blow; or who should take his Head from his Shoulders most cleverly; or who should run a man through after the most artificial manner." God doesn't require men to receive his Word on such hard terms, Bartholomew tells the king. He concludes the work with an essay called "The Art of Travelling," which among other things offers a string of suggestions about how his countrymen might go into foreign lands in ways that would render them something other than total barbarians, despised by all.

Others would come to the New World who, while refraining from killing Indians for sport, were more than willing to do so as part of a somber effort to clear a path through the wilderness for God's chosen people. Of these there could hardly be a better example than the Puritans, who, while thoroughly committed to staking a life in the wilds, were at the same time sorely lacking in enthusiasm. What was the use of climbing the heights, lamented William Bradford in his dreary *Of Plymouth Plantation,* when there was nothing to see but "a hideous and desolate wilderness, full of wild beasts and wild men." Why bother gaining the summit of Mount Pisgah since whichever way you turned your eyes—"save upward to the heavens"—there was nothing in the way of solace or content. Always on guard against temptation, Puritan leaders invested a remarkable amount of energy in making sure the flock didn't stray, in large part because of what they considered to be the corrupting influences of the Indians. Granted, these leaders were well aware that much of the enlightenment of their own heroes—John the Baptist, Ezekiel, Amos, even Christ himself—depended on privations endured in wild country. Yet the mainstream faithful were hardly as capable of warding off temptations, leading church leaders to conclude that wild country and its inhabitants were best avoided at all costs. In Connecticut, leaving the village and heading off into the woods to hang out with Indians could cost you a sound whipping, three years in prison, and a substantial fine.

Which makes even more intriguing those Puritans who

were simply too fascinated by such surroundings to resist heading out for a closer look. English lawyer Thomas Morton, for one, thought it very much worth heading up to the summit of Pisgah, where he saw things rather differently than his gloomy contemporary William Bradford. "The more I looked, the more I liked it. And when I had more seriously considered of the beauty of the place, with all her fair endowments, I did not think that in all the knowne world it could be paralleled. . . . If this land be not rich, then is the whole world poor." Morton not only had the gall to become friends with the Indians but engaged in regular trade with them. In time the native people became frequent visitors to his settlement at Merry Mount, populated in large part by waifs, strays, and others who found themselves at odds with Puritan leaders. On one occasion in 1627 Morton threw a kind of colonial rave, erecting a maypole on the summit of Merry Mount and decorating it with stag bells and brightly colored strips of cloth, dancing and frolicking with his friends, which again included many Indians. Puritan leaders were not amused. Morton was arrested and exiled to England, his colony disbanded.

This squeamishness toward the natives was at the heart of a sharp hostility toward French trappers, who'd long been forging successful fur-trading ventures by building close associations with Indians, routinely marrying and living with the tribes. A century later Frenchmen would make up fully one-half of all trappers in the Rockies—again showing a fondness for working and living closely with the natives, and again earning contempt for it. Such relationships became even more untenable as politicians began co-opting religious rhetoric to shore up their political ambitions in the West. Determined to exploit the riches of the Rockies and the lands beyond, one expansionist policy after another was launched, each tied to specific interpretations of the Bible— in particular, an old favorite that cast Anglos as the chosen people. When John Quincy Adams called for a westward expansion into Oregon in 1846, his argument rested on the need to "increase, multiply and subdue the earth, which we are commanded to do by the first behest of God Almighty." Likewise powerful senator Thomas Hart Benton was able to stump for manifest destiny in openly racist fashion. The white race alone, he advised, "had received the Devine command to subdue and replenish the earth. For it is the only race that . . . hunts out new and distant lands, and even a New World, to subdue and replenish." Even the official names first plastered on much of the Rocky Mountain landscape—many of them long since changed—tended to reinforce notions of good white folks conquering evil places. For a time valleys, rock slides, and various peaks and promontories were littered with references to Satan, hell, and the devil. In 1850 Father DeSmet told his followers that Indians near Yellowstone believed that the thermal features were heated by evil spirits who were "continually at the anvil forging their weapons." Never mind that at the time the Indians of that region had scant knowledge of blacksmithing. Likewise one observer, though enjoying greatly the strange rock formations at the Garden of the Gods, near Colorado Springs, lamented that "something less heathenish [for a name] would have better befitted these Christian days." (Hopefully this author never came across accounts of one rock formation in particular at the Garden of the Gods, said to resemble a seal making love to a nun.)

MANIFEST DESTINY required leaders not only willing to speak out against close relationships with Indians but also willing to ignore native accomplishments. And there was plenty to overlook. Writing systems had been in use for centuries by the Iroquois, Navajo, Sioux, Apache, Cherokee, Yaqui, and many others. As researchers Daniel Littlefield and James Parins point out, between 1772 and 1924 more than 6,700 pieces of English-language work were published by two thousand Native American writers, few of which have even been recognized, let alone discussed by popular historians. In the years between 1828 to 1924 Native Americans founded or edited more than fifty newspapers, beginning with the *Cherokee Phoenix* in Georgia; by 1900 a person would've been hard pressed to find a town anywhere in Indian Territory (a stretch of land including present-day Oklahoma) that didn't have at least one paper, with most larger native communities offering at least one daily.

In 1826 Tuscarora Indian David Cusick published his *Ancient History of the Six Nations;* by the time the Civil War broke out Ojibwa writers William Warren, George Copway, and Peter Jones had all produced histories of their people. Along the way there'd been an abundance of personal journals, polemics, and public addresses—some dealing with the land itself, others turning on themes of native identity and tribal sovereignty. Other, far older record-keeping traditions were thriving as well—from the Dakota winter counts of the Plains tribes, used to convey history via paintings on buffalo robes, to complex biographical records by the interior Salish, fashioned from knot clusters tied into lengths of string.

Natives routinely guided colonists and explorers toward useful edible and medicinal plants (indeed, by the early twentieth century almost half the world's domesticated food crops were ones first cultivated by the Indians of the Americas, including corn, potatoes, beans, peanuts, squash, and tomatoes). Throughout most of the nineteenth century, natives in so-called Indian Territory had flourishing educational systems, not to mention economic and intertribal councils that routinely gave advice to tribes throughout the East. More overlooked still is their knack for creative government. Long before Columbus stumbled ashore in the New World, the Iroquois had a written constitution featuring such democratic concepts as suffrage, recall procedures, and referendums. Benjamin Franklin, for one, was well aware of the Iroquois system—so much so that some historians suggest he may have used it as a rough blueprint for a version of Federalism for the United States. As one contemporary of Franklin's put it, the Iroquois had "outdone the Romans." At the height of the populist movement of the

1920s, when large numbers of Americans were once again fed up with corporate abuse, popular naturalist Ernest Thompson Seton wrote in *Current Opinion* that the Indians' government might be a worthwhile alternative. "The Indian solved the one great economic problem that vexes us today. By his life and tribal constitution, he has shown us that the nationalization of all natural resources and national interests puts a stop at once equally to abject poverty and to monstrous wealth."

Again, it wasn't merely a lack of interest that kept preachers, politicians, and even historians from turning to such sources for clues about native cultures. The plain fact was that the details of those lives contradicted completely the powerful mythology that drove much of the official activity in the Rockies and West: namely, the idea that our progress, indeed our very destiny as a nation, depended on placing both land and Indians in direct opposition to civilization. (Perhaps not surprisingly, much the same can be said for blacks. Rocky Mountain trapper Jim Beckwourth's autobiography, for example, published by Harper & Brothers in 1856, was quickly dismissed as the rantings of a mongrel.) Native cultures were seen as a part of the wild, not just as fodder for our heartbroken fantasies of the noble savage; more significantly, relegating an entire race to nature meant that it was part of the creation over which God himself was said to have given us total control. Even that most famous of American nature boys, Henry David Thoreau, would show himself highly critical of Native Americans. "What a coarse and imperfect use Indians and hunters make of Nature! No wonder that their race is so soon exterminated."

Besides having the support of mountain men, the tribes also tended to fare well in their dealings with artists. George Catlin headed west to the Rockies in 1830, six years before the first immigrants hit the Oregon Trail, on a somewhat desperate mission to make portraits of a way of life that even then he perceived as being overwhelmed by the whites. His hope, he explained, was to snatch "from a hasty oblivion what could be saved for the benefit of posterity . . . as a fair and just monument to the memory of a truly lofty and noble race." For seven years Catlin journeyed back and forth between St. Louis and the mountains, not just creating paintings of the Indians but assembling reams of notes and sketches about the cultures he encountered. The resulting gallery—the first to depict native cultures west of the Mississippi, including Pawnee, Sioux, Assiniboin, Blackfeet, Comanche, and Crow—was greeted with enormous enthusiasm by many in the general public, remaining on nearly constant exhibit for fourteen years.

Yet despite strong efforts by powerful people (not to mention unanimous support from the Committee on Indian Affairs), no one was able to convince the government to purchase Catlin's work, even though at the time such acquisitions were routine. The artist himself had little doubt as to the reason, blaming President Andrew Jackson, who he claimed had launched nothing less than a conspiracy against the Indians. As part of his so-called Indian Removal Policy

Jackson had already cleared most tribes from the south—a move meant to "enable those States to advance rapidly in population, wealth, and power," and at the same time "allow the Indians to cast off their savage habits and become an interesting, civilized, and Christian community." Catlin cast the policy in a different light, describing it as an underhanded way to facilitate the placement of slaves needed to work the southern cotton crops. By 1837 nearly every tribe in the East, South, and Midwest had been relocated to lands west of the Mississippi and Arkansas Rivers. Thus a barrier had been created, Jackson explained, contradicting his earlier remarks, "for their protection against the encroachment of our citizens, guarding [them] as far as possible from those evils which have brought them to their present condition." Besides, offered the president, it could hardly be supposed "that the wandering savage has a stronger attachment to his home than the settled, civilized Christian."

This age-old willingness to place God in service of empire has always brought with it tremendous potential for harming a culture's most cherished principles. The destruction of tribal governments in Indian country following the Civil War was by any standard of democracy appalling. Despite overwhelming evidence that many of these native cultures not only were highly accomplished but had long ago organized around systems that fit easily into the accepted definition of legitimate government, American courts had thirty years earlier refused to grant sovereignty to Indian republics, determining them to be instead "domestic dependent nations," as Chief Justice John Marshall described them. Destroying the structure of a tribe was considered not an offense against a sovereign nation, but rather a simple matter of internal policy. The reason Indians were so fiercely opposed to becoming U.S. citizens is because with citizenship came implicit permission for the American government to gain "legal" control of their lands.

In this atmosphere even science found itself in the service of degrading the Indian. By 1850 noted scientist Samuel George Morton had given what many considered irrefutable evidence of polygenism, a belief that different races not only varied considerably in intelligence but were in fact different species. His conclusions were based on having measured cranial capacities—and therefore, he explained, intellectual capacity—of some six hundred skulls from various races. This in turn led to a ranking of the races, which Morton said were led by Caucasians, followed by people of Mongolian and Malay descent. At the bottom of the list were Native Americans and blacks. Morton went on to combine his data with reports of the attributes of various races, most of it taken from travel literature, and from this witches' brew concluded the Native American to be "averse to cultivation, and slow in acquiring knowledge; restless, revengeful and fond of war." Though the flaws in Morton's cranial project would today outrage the most uninspired high school student (his measurements failed to take even gender or body size into consideration), the research was eagerly embraced by those with their fingers on the buttons of myth. It added considerable energy to the feeling of inevitability that attended the westward movement, fueling a notion that we were being led across the mountains by an eternal truth of both God and nature.

OUTSIDE THE SENATE ENTRANCE of the U.S. Capitol building is a massive panel of carvings by nineteenth-century artist Thomas Crawford—some eighty feet long and twelve feet high at the center—called *Progress of Civilization*. In the right section of the work is a cluster of panels that serve as the perfect visual bite for this prevailing attitude toward native people, perspectives that were playing out in the Rockies even as Crawford stood with chisel in hand. At the left edge of this run of panels is the image of a stalwart backwoodsman surrounded by stumps, along with a rattlesnake hightailing it for safer pastures. To the right of this is the figure of an Indian, the son of a chief, carrying on his shoulder a spear heavy with game, looking with surprise toward the woodsman with the ax. Beside him, in turn, is his father, the chief, also looking back on the scene of the pioneer, but with an expression of great sadness. "In the statue of the Indian chief," wrote Crawford of his work, "I have endeavored to concentrate all the despair and profound grief resulting from the conviction of the white man's triumph." The chief is joined on the panel by his wife and infant son; beside them is a grave, which Crawford explains as being emblematic of the extinction of the Indian race.

In the years following Crawford's work there would be plenty of other eulogies for the natives of the Rockies, many of them from travel writers. Having waxed poetic about the range in *The Switzerland of America*, Samuel Bowles offers in 1869 a no-nonsense summary of the decline of the Indian, preselling what sounds very much like the guts of so-called social Darwinism. "His game flies before the white man; we cannot restore it to him if we would; we would not if we could. It is his destiny to die. We cannot continue him to his original, barbaric life; he cannot mount that of civilization. The mongrel marriage of the two that he embraces and must submit to, is killing him—and all we can do is to smooth and make decent the path to his grave."

Meanwhile official boosters of the Rockies, including many Territorial Immigration Boards, were doing everything possible to get rid of the Indians, all the while concocting promotional material with pens dipped in honey so as to not offend eastern sensibilities. In 1874, two years before Custer was sent to his Maker on the hills above the Greasy Grass, officials in Colorado Territory were struggling mightily to calm the fears of those considering a move to the Rockies. "The savages, who in years past roamed over the plains have, through military persuasion, been happily translated to their 'eternal hunting grounds,' are securely cooped up within their military reservations, under the surveillance of the military, and are as subdued as little children."

Again, such history seems weightier by virtue of what most felt was the sheer inevitability of it. That there should be another approach to dealing with native populations, allowing at least the structures of traditional native government, was an idea most leaders considered absurd. On a trip to the Rockies around 1839—in the last flush of the mountain man era, but long before either mad rushes for gold or major conflicts with western Indians—Dr. F. A. Wislizenus wrote a cynical yet thoroughly accurate view of the future of the Rocky Mountain tribes.

> So the waves of civilization will draw nearer and nearer from the East and from the West, till they cover the sandy plains, and cast their spray on the feet of the Rockies. The few fierce tribes who may have maintained themselves until that time in the mountains, may offer some resistance to the progress of the waves, but the swelling flood will rise higher and higher, till at last they are buried beneath it. The buffalo and the antelope will be buried with them; and the bloody tomahawk will be buried too. But for all that there will be no smoking of the pipe of peace; for the new generation with the virtues of civilization will bring also its vices. It will ransack the bowels of the mountains to bring to light the most precious of all metals, which, when brought to the light, will arouse strife and envy and all ignoble passions, and the sons of civilization will be no happier than their red brethren who have perished.

Had we turned even occasionally to stories from the Indians themselves, we would have found in many cases images of societies much less naïve than our own—people who embraced the notion that beauty and chaos stood side by side. Native stories from the Rockies speak of the promise of abundant spring harvests in the camas fields. Or of times of war, when the tribal identity of a man on horseback could be determined from a half mile away by nothing more than the rider's posture. They are stories of movement: treks east to the plains of Montana to hunt buffalo, west to acquire trade goods, and, in the eighteenth century, south past the southern reaches of the range to procure horses from the Spanish. There are images of ships coming into northwestern ports along the Pacific loaded with precious hawk beads from Belgium, vermilion dye from China, wool from England—and the coast itself, rich in shells highly valued by tribes a thousand miles to the east. And goods flowing in the opposite direction as well, away from the Rockies—obsidian for arrow points taken from the heart of Yellowstone, as well as furs and other animal parts, plants for dyes and medicines, pipestone and earth paints, quillwork and clays. Before the advent of British and American forts, obtaining such goods meant either trading with other tribes—some of whom might be enemies at other times of the year—or making ambitious treks to the source, a kind of commercial hopscotch spanning much of the continent. Indeed no trapper, no government explorer (including the government's favorite son, the so-called pathfinder Charles Fremont), failed to take their cues from routes established centuries before by native hunters and traders.

One little-known account of such a journey was written by a Nez Perce woman known only as Catherine, who recalled a remarkable trading excursion she made as a girl around 1841 with a large entourage of trappers, traveling from Montana's Big Hole River south along the Rockies to the Green River, then west along the Colorado River all the way to the Pacific. Some two thousand miles in all, much of it with enough drama to leave modern readers exhausted at the mere thought of it. "An old and new life was around me on foot and on wing, an old and new life in leaf and blade," she writes of a spring day early in the journey. "The earth required more space. The sky grew higher with the sun. The wild striped little honey bee that hides his two stands of honey in the rents of the mountain rocks was at work, and as I rode aside and alone his moans made me sadder, and I wondered if I would ever return."

The trip began in the season of high waters; on reaching a stream some seventy paces wide, Catherine tells of the women stripping to cotton shirts and tying their children onto their backs, then lightening the saddles on their best horses and swimming alongside their mounts to the other side—one by one, until the entire family was across. Catherine bore her little brother while her sister rode strapped to the back of her stepmother. The water was cold, she writes, fresh from the high peaks and parent springs, and by the end of the ferry their hands and limbs were as "red as the wild roses" from the chill. There were nights dark and moonless, she tells us, yet cloudless, when the stars were as close together as the buds on the bush of the mountain berry.

"My father, who was a brave and cautious man, always advised me on his travels to be on the watch, my eyes being young and strong. Mountains and plains, the sky, sun and buffalo. Just as far as the earnest eye could see until the sky struck the earth I could see nothing but buffalo and the other smaller game lost in their masses, like young children with the group camps." As in all such forays, the party was at various times traveling in enemy territory. The great difficulty, Catherine says of the stress she felt in such places, came down to the matter of wakefulness. Particularly at night, "when it dyes the brain and leaves one with a want of serenity, when appetite is lost and even the brave become fools. Callousness succeeds and frequently if the enemy were on hand he could count his victims with stones."

In what is now western Colorado the party was in fact attacked by an enemy tribe. Desperate for some sense of how to battle an unfamiliar foe, in the heat of the battle a young unnamed black trapper traveling with the group asked Catherine for advice. Tell your friend, she said, pointing to a rather famous redheaded mountain man named Baker, "excellent at his weapon," to shoot the chief with the black star on his chest—the one who at that very moment was crawling toward them on all fours like a dog. This posture, she explained to the young black man, was something warriors of that tribe did when deciding trials of life or death. "The combat depends now upon his life and he makes the dog as of old to win or lose it," she told him, the pair moving quickly to Baker's side. A moment later redheaded Baker, raising his gun to take aim at this chief, now some forty paces away, accidentally hit Catherine in the forehead with the stock of his rifle, causing a bleeding wound. "I said in my heart," Catherine recalls of the moment, " 'That star will die!' for in desperate times I often found that our minds see and decide ahead of our bodies, like a beam preceding the sun before he is up." Sure enough, Baker positioned his rifle and sent a lead ball into the head of the chief, killing him instantly. The next morning, with at least half of their horses and mules dead and their leaders and many of their best men slain, Catherine's group limped back toward the Colorado River and resumed their journey.

From this point Catherine's story becomes a string of matter-of-fact details: certain members of the party stealing children from other tribes to sell to the Spaniards; executions by trappers of impoverished natives whom they accused of having stolen beaver traps along the lower Colorado; times when horses had to be shot in order to make hide boats for crossing dangerous rivers. And a particularly memorable day when the group stumbled across several abandoned children along the lower Colorado, choked with fear. Thanks to careful attention by Catherine and others, their alarm eventually wore off, and as the days passed they once again became playful. "The Restorer, time, grew upon them as every day told how glad and brief and bitter are our seasons."

Like other denizens of the Rockies, the native peoples of this region have long been considered less real people

than agents of myth. Many assigned them the role of inferior, godless creatures—the evil that Christianity needed
desperately to struggle against if it was to make whole the
barrens of the West, the heathen enemy that made manifest
destiny seem not just reasonable but obligatory. Others,
meanwhile, would come to favor instead the noble savage
image, attempting to fill some lost, wild furrow in our own
identity that became precious exactly at the point it drifted
out of reach.

C H A P T E R 5

Lords, Farmers, and
Other Tourists

Stewart's Camp, Lake, Wind River Mountains (1865)

ALFRED JACOB MILLER

Alfred Jacob Miller, artistic companion to the wealthy Scottish traveler Sir
William Drummond Stewart, proved one of the great chroniclers of the
post–fur trade era. This work, which was prepared in part from sketches
made during a visit to the New Fork Lakes, near the headwaters of the
Green River, shows a strong influence by the French Romantics.

MIDMORNING, EARLY SUMMER OF 1843, east of the Rockies on the windswept plains near Chokecherry Creek. Friedrich Armand Strubberg has been gone from civilization for more than a year. Though well educated, like most of his fellow wanderers he's got little sense of what's been going on in the world at large. Has no clue about the sensational new book *A Christmas Carol,* by Charles Dickens. Knows nothing about Wordsworth being named poet laureate. Is unfamiliar with the breakthrough discovery of anesthetic, about the growing fight along the eastern seaboard to improve working conditions for women. Strubberg is likely even unaware that a swarm of a thousand emigrants have left St. Louis, heading west by wagon on the Oregon Trail. To him the world has slowed to a walk, any given day bringing only a handful of possibilities: thunderstorms rising in the afternoon to stab the prairie with lightning, the ground rumbling with the hooves of bison. The Sioux or the Mandan suddenly appearing, gliding down from the hills quiet as ghosts, eyeing suspiciously the few cattle he has in tow. But for that, life is monotonous, monastic, as rhythmic as breathing.

This day, though, brings something different. Peering over a small rise in the middle of a prairie nowhere, Strubberg sees in the distance what at first seems like a mirage. Dozens of tents are pitched in the cradles of the hills, brightly colored flags atop the center poles snapping in the breeze. Milling about are fifty or so men and roughly a hundred horses and mules. Some of the party are dawdling, ambling toward the nearby stream to wash the sleep from their eyes, while others pass bottles of whiskey around the breakfast fires. Fastening a handkerchief to the end of his rifle, Strubberg fires both barrels, is waved in with enthusiasm. As he moves closer, suddenly aware of his shabby clothes stained with grease and blood, he makes out what appears to be a traveling circus or a costume ball—"the most curious army I ever beheld." A nineteenth-century equivalent of the barroom scene in *Star Wars*.

There on the banks of the stream are natives in breechcloth and gentlemen in smoking jackets. Others are dressed in medieval fashions, including jerkins with slit sleeves and plumed hats, velvet paletots from old Spain, the chapeaus of old Italian brigand chiefs. Some of the men sport red feathers above their long coiffed hair, with white linen shirts turned down at the collar. A handful are apparently fans of James Fenimore Cooper's Leatherstocking tales, dressed as they are in leather from head to toe with long hunting knives on their belts, unwieldy rifles at their sides. Elsewhere large spurs rattle on red Moroccan boots. There are even men in slippers, manicured fingers wrapped around Cuban cigars.

In the center of the commotion is the apparent ringmaster of the group, talking loudly to a bunch of eager listeners, someone who seems vaguely familiar. On hearing the man's Scottish brogue, it dawns on Strubberg that he's met this energetic man before, some ten years earlier. Lord William Drummond Stewart, wealthy gentry from Scotland on his way to the Rockies—if not the black sheep of his family, then a dark gray one for sure. The next two days are for Strubberg like a good dream. "The most delicious wines graced our table which was covered by artistic cooks with the daintiest dishes. We smoked the best cigars and drank the best mocha. We spent time in firing at a mark, in riding races, in various sports, card playing and dicing, in hunting. . . . [O]ur pipes burnt incessantly, brandy was often mixed with our water, we had coffee to drink, our meat was peppered and salted, biscuits were eaten with it, and before going to bed we had a glass of grog; and these things now afforded double enjoyment after the lengthened privation."

William Drummond Stewart had made other treks to the Rocky Mountains. In 1833, for the sum of five hundred dollars, he was allowed to hitch a ride with fur traders William Sublette and Robert Campbell; despite some hair-raising experiences, he stayed on for several years. Following that knockabout came a winter in New Orleans, after which he heard the mountains calling again, and so set off for another six-month journey—this time with a young artist from Baltimore in tow named Alfred Jacob Miller, destined to become one of the most celebrated illustrators of his time. Stewart, incidentally, wasn't the first rich man to travel with an artist; in the early 1830s Prince Maximilian journeyed up the Missouri with the stellar German painter Karl Bodmer. But while Bodmer's charge was in large part anthropological, Stewart was happy merely to have someone along to capture key moments of the adventure, lugging Miller along like later vacationers might cart a Kodak, recording scenes to inspire the Scotsman when he returned to his far more sedate, somewhat forlorn life on the other side of the Atlantic. Miller left the field with some two hundred sketches in hand. These he later turned into paintings that not only garnered tremendous acclaim in the galleries of Baltimore and New York but gave the public their best look yet at the Rocky Mountains and its trappers. In time, though, the works ended up right where Stewart intended all along, hanging on the walls of his palatial home at Murthly Castle in Perthshire, near the Burnham Wood.

Stewart's earlier forays had spoiled him. He complained often to friends that the Rockies made subsequent travels in Russia and the Orient feel tame by comparison. Aged fifty, hungry for one more fling in the high country, in 1843 he set up a final trip to the Rockies, selling the journey as adventure travel to some two dozen men from throughout the East and Midwest. He had no trouble filling the slots. In a letter to the *Savannah Republican,* an unnamed member of the group describes the party as consisting of about twenty gentlemen and some thirty servants. The greatest number, he concluded, "seem to have no other object than to spend a pleasant summer, and improve their constitution by exposure to hot and cold, rainy and dry weather." Included in the group were numerous men of science, including four botanists, two ornithologists, and two doctors (complete with the latest fracture machine "and all the other instruments of torture" belonging to the profession). Despite the privations involved with a six-month journey into rugged country, most thought the whole affair rather plush. "It is an elegant way of living we have in this far west," wrote a reporter named Richard Rowland in a letter to his sister. "Here is Sir William, as rich as a Santa Fe nabob, traveling about, talking Indian, and looking like Robinson Crusoe."

Also along for the ride was the nineteen-year-old son of explorer William Clark, who'd bid farewell to his father in St. Louis with his own horse and personal manservant. Caring for the draft animals, meanwhile, was none other than Baptiste Charbonneau, son of Sacagawea. For a portion of the trip even John James Audubon rode along, a man who despite his remarkable travels throughout much of America had grown increasingly frustrated at having missed out on the West. Audubon planned to meet up with Stewart in St. Louis, who was traveling by steamship from New Orleans, then continue on with his party up the Missouri River to the Yellowstone. The steamship wrecked just south of the city, costing Stewart not just his equipment but his faith in steamboats; in a matter of hours he decided to abandon the water route and make for the Rockies overland instead. Though Stewart apologized to Audubon for the change of plans—offering him five mules and a wagon for the journey across the plains—it wasn't enough to entice the great artist, who at fifty-eight was already in marginal health. "I am told he would give a great deal to have us join him," Audubon wrote to his wife. "If so, why does he not offer some ten thousand dollars? Who knows but that in such a case I might venture to leap on a mule's back and trot some seven or eight thousand miles." Audubon continued upriver on the Missouri, eventually catching up with the group and traveling contentedly with them for many miles. Audubon was "a great man," wrote Richard Rowland, "and one of the few white ones that ever made traveling in this part of the world advantageous to himself and his country."

A century later, historians would describe the Stewart trek as the first tourist trip to Wyoming. In truth, it was more like a wacky version of the Grand Tour—that famous rite of passage for well-heeled children of Europeans and Brits, who followed up formal education with extended rambles to key sites in Europe. When it first began, the Grand Tour was mostly concerned not with landscapes but with art and antiquity, though some did get the chance to thrill to the sight of Mount Vesuvius erupting. Such travelers had a special fondness for archaeological digs, especially in Italy, where they watched in amazement as ancient treasures were plucked from the earth before their very eyes, rarely suspecting that these were often staged events. Stewart and the boys no doubt thought themselves to be doing the Europeans one better. Their party, after all, would in their encounters with natives be seeing not just remnants of old cultures but the cultures themselves, generally intact, going about the business of everyday living. Which on any given day could include the firing of real arrows at uninvited tourists. This proud dismissal of European tourist attractions in favor of the natural wonders of America would continue for another fifty years. Writing to his cousin about a trip to Yellowstone in 1908, for example, A. S. Custer from Cincinnati displays an unabashed loyalty to his homeland. "The only thing in which Europe excels is in her ancient ruins and volcanoes. If we want old ruins we will build them, and as for Mt. Vesuvius, if we had the troublesome thing in this country we would turn Niagara Falls into it and put it out of commission in ten minutes."

In the lead guide slot for the 1843 expedition was trapper William Sublette, the same man who nearly froze to death twenty years earlier near the Wind River Range on the Popo Agie while traveling with fellow trapper James Clyman. Having for years suffered from poor health, Sublette roused himself for the chance to take the lead in guiding this peculiar group of tourists into the mountains he loved. Sublette had shortly before helped build Fort Laramie with Robert Campbell and Black Harris, a place that fast became the crossroads of the world for aging mountain men. Drifting through at all hours was a who's who of the trapping world, from James Beckwourth to Jim Bridger, Hugh Glass to "Broken Hand" Fitzpatrick. Men not only highly regarded for their wilderness skills, but who by their very presence in the Rockies and Far West had—just as Jefferson hoped—become a front guard in the effort to break English occupation in the Pacific Northwest.

As part of that effort, in 1830 Jedediah Smith, David Jackson, and William Sublette had written a letter to secre-

tary of war John Eaton urging him to push for the termina-
tion of the Convention of 1818 between Great Britain and
the United States. While the boundary between Canada and
the United States was set at the 49th parallel, under this
convention it was decided that any land claimed by either
country "on the North West Coast of America, westward of
the Stony Mountains [the Rockies], shall, together with it's
Harbours, Bays, and Creeks, and the Navigation of all
Rivers within the same, be free and open, for the term of ten
Years from the date of the Signature of the present Convention, to the Vessels, Citizens, and Subjects of the Two Powers." In 1828 that most intrepid of mountain men Jedediah
Smith reached the Hudson Bay post of Fort Vancouver, on
the north side of the Columbia, about five miles above the
mouth of the Multnomah River—today's Willamette River
in Oregon. There he found impressive crops of wheat, corn,
barley, and peas, two hundred cattle and three hundred hogs,
even saw mills and grist mills. More to the point, Smith estimated the annual harvest of beaver pelts being taken from
U.S. territory to be worth more than a quarter of a million
dollars. "Every thing seemed to combine to prove," said
Smith and his partners in their letter to Eaton, "that this fort
was to be a permanent establishment." Unless the British
were stopped, the territory would soon be exhausted of
beaver, "and no place left within the United States where
beaver fur in any quantity can be obtained." (Never mind the
frenzied pace of harvest being simultaneously engineered by
the Americans.) Beyond urging the repeal of the Conven-

tion of 1818, the trappers argued that the best way to stop such intrusions in the future would be to start filling the region with Americans, who they were convinced could cross the continent with wagons from St. Louis to the Great Falls of the Columbia. It was a feat they'd already proven feasible, after all, crossing the Rockies in present-day Wyoming at South Pass.

Stewart's traveling circus crossed the Missouri River on May 20, 1843, hitting the Kansas prairies immediately ahead of another, far larger group of around a thousand people. This emigrant wagon train, bound for Oregon, had been organized by popular missionary Dr. Marcus Whitman. Whitman had come west seven years earlier—among the first to navigate the Oregon Trail by wagon—and gone on to set up missions in the Northwest with his wife Narcissa, as well as friends and fellow missionaries Henry and Eliza Spalding. Narcissa and Eliza were in fact the first Anglo women to cross the Rockies, cresting South Pass on the Fourth of July, 1836, escorted by none other than African-American mountain man "Black Harris." Reaction by natives to the women's presence had been striking. "We ladies were such a curiosity to them," wrote Narcissa. "They would come and stand around our tent, peep in, and grin in their astonishment to see such strange looking objects." Having descended South Pass, the party reached the Green River near Horse Creek. Here they came upon the annual rendezvous, a revolving hullabaloo jump-started by William Ashley of the Rocky Mountain Fur Company in 1825 as a commercial gathering for mountain men, Indians, and merchants who supplied equipment for the trapping trade. Pelts were exchanged, supplies purchased, horse races run and shooting contests held, massive quantities of alcohol consumed, wives lost and found—a kind of no-holds-barred fraternity party with guns. Yet here too Narcissa Whitman reports being met by a large company of native matrons, "one after another shaking hands and saluting me with a most hearty kiss."

The mountain men too proved eager to meet the women, though their welcome was decidedly more raucous. As the wagons approached, trapper Joe Meek and a dozen or so Indian and Anglo compadres crested the brow of a hill with a white flag raised, riding and zagging toward the missionaries with incredible speed and daring, dashing along the wagon train shouting and screaming, finally discharging their guns over the heads of the startled party. Only the calming reassurances of the guide prevented a full-blown panic. Despite being apprehensive about the trappers, when they were in the presence of the women the missionaries found them gentle to a fault—showing, as Henry Spaulding put it, "the greatest kindness throughout the whole journey. We have wanted nothing which was in their power to furnish us." Meek seemed downright smitten with Narcissa, spending long hours either riding with her or parked in front of her tent, regaling her with stories of life in the Rockies.

Despite great conviction, things would end up going badly for the Whitmans at their mission in Washington's

Walla Walla Valley. Many of the Cayuse Indians they'd been charged with saving remained unreceptive, perhaps in part because of Narcissa's unwillingness to grant any sort of legitimacy to existing Cayuse social and religious practices. The long-standing native tradition of giving away personal possessions, for example, she wrote off as extortion. The situation worsened until finally the American Missionary Board decided in 1842 to close the mission. Undaunted, Marcus made the long trek back east to cajole the board to keep the doors open, returning in 1843 with this massive group of emigrants, trailing right behind William Drummond Stewart.

In truth it was a lousy slot in the parade. Stewart's group, though small, was made up of men obsessed with hunting; across hundreds of miles of prairie they kept scattering the game six ways to Sunday, just ahead of Whitman's party, often making it impossible for the faithful to find enough food. Out in front, Stewart was having no such problems. Near Scott's Bluff the party ran into what was for most the greatest wildlife spectacle of their lives, described with great flare by William Clark Kennerly, nephew of explorer William Clark:

> Far out on the Platte one morning, while making preparations for our daily hunt, we descried coming toward us a herd [of buffalo], which I can state without any exaggeration must have numbered a million. The pounding of their hooves on the hard prairie sounded like the roaring of a mighty ocean,

surging over the land and sweeping everything before it. Here was more game than we bargained for, and the predicament in which we now found ourselves gave us much cause for alarm. On they came, and as we were directly in their path and on the bank of the river, there was great danger of our being swept over.

The party avoided that danger only with difficulty, resorting to desperate measures to turn the herd. Guards were posted, charged with waving their arms and shouting at the animals at the top of their lungs. At night the men lit enormous bonfires. Though moving "at quite a rapid gate," it took two full days for the animals to pass.

Despite his penchant for traveling with everything but the kitchen sink, Stewart wasn't exactly a cruise director for the faint of heart. Crossing a dangerous, rain-swollen Kansas River on horseback years before with Alfred Jacob Miller, mid-stream Stewart had asked the nervous artist if he knew how to swim. Miller replied that he did not. Me neither, Stewart admitted, then went on to explain that this was the way a man built self-reliance, that you can never know what you can do until you try. Later in the journey, on a particularly dreary day on the prairies, Stewart was shocked to find Miller feeling down in the dumps. He chided the young artist, told him that his early training must have been faulty—that days of fine weather were nowhere near as exhilarating as days when weather was foul, the latter being something to compete against. Time and again

Stewart proved quick to follow his nose into any situation that promised the slightest intrigue.

On the other hand, during evening hours Stewart's camps displayed all the qualities of a wilderness salon. Writing to his father from the rendezvous of 1836, William F. Kline offers a wonderful glimpse into the more cerebral aspects of what it was like hanging out with the crazy Scotsman:

> I have had the pleasure and honor of being an invited guest of Sir William Drummond Stewart, a captain in Her Majesty's British Life Guards. During the Rendezvous, Captain Stewart hosts an exclusive camp of his own, usually up some tributary away from all the raucous of the trappers and traders, inviting men of experience and knowledge. For many days, this group of individuals hold a type of court under a canvas canopy large enough to sit two dozen men. Here we have the opportunity to hear from scientists of all natures; men who study the history of rocks, the plants, the insects and animals. Even the paths of the stars in the night sky. This unique gathering is a council of the wise. I felt less separated from the civilized world while in the company of these men. During the afternoons, I will read the newspapers you have sent me to the audience and then open the rest of the time until dark to discussion of the current events. We philosophize all subjects, it seems to exhaustion, and then supper is served. The mornings of our days at Captain Stewart's camp are usually taken up in short excursions touring

the nearby area. We have found canyons containing the fossils of long ago creatures. Uncatalogued species of plants and insects seem too numerous to count. We have come across sacred and holy places, filling us with awe and tranquility, places where no living thing is permitted; places so silent and empty they must be openings to other dimensions and levels of existence.

Such dispatches and letters home make the Stewart trip of 1843 especially valuable. Many party members wrote regular summaries of the experience, including an accomplished newspaperman and former actor named Matthew Field. On contracting tuberculosis Field had in 1839 quit the theater and headed west to Santa Fe. Along the way he sent articles back to the *New Orleans Picayune*—usually submitted under the bizarre pseudonym "Phazma"—giving readers some of the earliest and best popular accounts of the southern Rockies. He did the same with Stewart in 1843. While Field was clearly enamored of the lands beyond the hundredth meridian, his relationship goes beyond either frontier boosterism or the typical salvation-in-the-wilderness story lines that continued to surface unchecked in the East. One didn't have to embellish, Matthew Field assured his readers, to come up with good copy about the West. "Strange and dangerous adventure, histories of mournful interest, wild and startling tales of trial, privation, misery, bravery, feasting, fasting, fighting, scalping, adverse transitions, revelry, rivalry, etc., all glowing in fresh and vivid colors, may be picked up by anybody who will carry a book and pencil in his pocket, thick as blackberries, among the men of the mountains and the white wanderers of the wilderness."

Field offered readers not so much scenery per se as tales of human passion and hardship set in the heart of wild and beautiful country. One day he wrote of stumbling across a hapless messenger trying to cross the mountains, nearly frozen to death, beating his frostbitten feet and body with a rifle to keep the blood flowing. At other times he chronicled how hard it was for mountain men to leave the Rockies, even as the fur trade era was clearly winding down. On the Green River the party came across well-known trapper Mark Head, who by his own account had been in the mountains for eight to ten years. (Head's stature among his peers swelled considerably when he became one of the first to "play dead" during a horrific mauling by a grizzly bear.) Near-death experiences notwithstanding, Matt Field notes that Head had not a shred of desire to ever again visit his old home in the states. "This close attachment to the wild and homeless life we must mention as a striking characteristic of the mountain man," Field told readers in New Orleans. "Nearly every one of them answered our questions on this point by asserting their strong attachment to mountain life, merely acknowledging their disposition to visit their white friends of their youth as a matter of curiosity, but by all means to return to their leathern lodges among the big rocks."

Another journalist along for the ride was Richard

Rowland, who identified himself to readers of the *Concordia Intellegencer* only as "P.O.F.," and who was christened "Little Woeful" by reporter Matt Field. "The other night we sat out all night in the rain, as our baggage took the wrong fork, which is a greater mistake . . . than taking the wrong tooth brush at a hotel. It would have done you good to see us enjoying ourselves out here, sitting Indian fashion, in a ring, soaked through and smoking all over, like rotten straw stirred up in a cold morning. . . . In my next [letter] I shall have passed above the Yellow Forks, and get into more interesting country, which will be a great relief to me—the great fault of the Far West being, that there is too much of it."

When, after nearly six months of travel—much of it roaming the Rockies of western Wyoming—the trip finally began to wind down, "Little Woeful" was saturated. He recounts one of the group's last meals—wild turkey "boiled dry as a chip," buffalo marrow for butter, bear ribs for pork, and prairie grouse christened as chicken. "To give the thing more the air of civilization, we all sat up bold, and in unnatural positions; and to make it still more 'white folks fashion,' we did not grease our faces in eating above our nose, and only used one hand when it was possible." There were toasts, a lot of them, and by the end of the night the whole party was stumbling about the prairie under dark skies, whistling "Auld Lang Syne." William Drummond Stewart looked around, raised his glass a final time to his companions. "Being out here is as much ahead of fiction as a sterling pound is worth more than a Scotch." As endorsements go this was a fairly mild one for Stewart—perhaps the effect of whiskey, mixed with the sadness of leaving. Far edgier comments are found in his journals, including the assertion that "to go back to civilized life and fight my way to every day's bread among the common herd would be worse than ten thousand deaths in heated blood here." When he did finally return to Scotland the aging nobleman found he could no longer sleep on the feather beds of Murthly Castle. Instead he curled up each night on a divan, covering himself with a large buffalo robe obtained on this final adventure in the West.

As a side note, that massive party of settlers missionary Marcus Whitman brought into Washington that same summer did nothing to improve relations with the Cayuse. In 1847 an epidemic of measles struck, and most of the white children lived while nearly all of the Cayuse children died. Suspecting foul play, on November 29 Chief Tiloukaikt took revenge, burning the mission and killing fourteen whites, including the Whitmans. Desperate to save some remnant of his tribe in the bloody war that followed, Tiloukaikt and several warriors surrendered to the whites two years later, his bravado undiminished. Standing on the gallows, he queried his executioners: "Did not your missionaries teach us that Christ died to save his people? So we die to save our people." Trapper Joe Meek—the man so taken with Narcissa Whitman at the Green River rendezvous in 1836—would later deliver the tragic news of her murder to her family in New York.

BY THE LATTER DECADES OF the nineteenth century the Rockies had become a powerful draw not just for wealthy travelers like Stewart but for families and common adventurers on shoestring budgets—all wandering the mountains on their own, not a guide or hunter or groomsman in sight. The journals, letters to relatives, and handful of magazine articles they left behind refute utterly the claims of authors who say nature preserves were in that era mostly playgrounds for the wealthy. Traveling in the northern Rockies in 1883, M. A. Cruikshank makes a special point of writing about her frequent encounters with families from across the region—farmers, ranchers, the occasional honeymooners. "We constantly met the most rustic of vehicles drawn by the roughest of farm animal, filled by the genuine sons and daughters of the soil. It was really strange to see how perfectly this class appreciate the wonders of the place and how glad they are to leave for a while their hard labor for the adventurous, the beautiful, and the sublime. They always carried their outfit, camping every night. I have no doubt that they saw more and enjoyed more than conventional travelers." Yet another observer in this same era, writing in the journal *Overland*, declared that "nowhere is rough-and-ready gypsy camping on the simplest scale more thoroughly appreciated as a family play than in the Western states."

One of Cruikshank's "daughters of the soil," Mrs. N. E. Cornell, traveled close to four hundred miles on a round-trip excursion to Yellowstone from her home in Laramie, Wyoming, in a spring wagon loaded with seven children.

She was the only adult. "Now if a timid mother with a wagonload of children (oldest boy not yet sixteen) can take the trip, anybody can, and everybody ought to. [The children] played in the Platte, the Sweetwater, the Popo Agie, the Wind, the Snake, the Yellowstone, Lewis, Firehole, Shoshone, Big Horn and Laramie Rivers. They have seen their native state as no books can teach it, and came home in the finest health with ravenous appetites." A Park Service report issued in 1911 estimates that roughly 50 percent of Yellowstone's visitors were local farmers and ranchers; indeed, acting park superintendent Lloyd Brett was strongly opposed to letting automobiles into Yellowstone National Park, in part because of the havoc they might wreak on families traveling by horse-drawn wagon. Likewise, two years earlier, acting superintendent Major H. C. Benson reported that out of some twenty thousand tourists in the park, probably not ten of the animals used had ever seen an automobile. Should motor vehicles be allowed, "a considerable number of the 20,000 visitors would either be killed, or injured . . . and the pleasure of every one of the 20,000 would be totally destroyed through fear."

Reports of such vacations suggest they were motivated less by a Teddy Roosevelt-style need to hone character (no doubt the daily demands of farming and ranching took care of that) than by a straightforward, altogether friendly curiosity toward any unique aspect of nature. Such travelers delighted not only in the beauty of the region, as Mrs. Cruikshank noted, but in how certain aspects of the wild could be easily employed to serve basic needs. Many were downright giddy at the chance to cook beans and potatoes in Yellowstone's hot pots, for example—though the uninitiated sometimes made the mistake of choosing a geyser instead of a hot pot, only to have the thing go off and send dinner rocketing across the landscape. Others were eager to find a certain fabled spot on the north shore of Yellowstone Lake, where it was said you could catch a fish and then—without taking a step or even removing it from the hook—drop it into a kind of geothermal Crock-Pot. As A. B. Guptill wrote in 1890, this was a most interesting feat, performed by many and witnessed by hundreds.

Margaret Andrews Allen, traveling with her family through Yellowstone in 1885, thrilled at what the Yellowstone country provided for those in need of clean laundry. "We have seen the only poetical washing-day in our lives," she writes after tossing her dirty dish towels into Castle Geyser for a thorough cleaning. "We wish all were like it. It's not turning the geyser into a base use; it is merely idealizing washing." Later on Margaret happened to spot people with bags of laundry dangling in hot pots at the ends of long poles, and immediately concluded the same could be done with food. "We have a ham in our wagon; why should not that be cooked in the same way? The Devil's Well is near, and soon our ham, in a strong sack fastened to a pole, is cheerfully bubbling away. In about two hours it is well done, and lasts us the rest of the journey."

As the twentieth century unfurled, improvements in

both the price and reliability of automobiles would offer locals of all stripes the chance to roam the Rockies behind a steering wheel. Not that even this sort of travel was easy. Whereas in 1930 the state of New York boasted more than ten thousand miles of hardtop roads, the state of Montana had less than a hundred. Just as dude ranches would attract eastern women who chafed at the conventions of high society, auto journeys through the mountains proved a perfect way for western women to move about on their own. Even Emily Post got into the act, traveling by car to the rural West in the spring of 1915, finding much there to appeal to the so-called weaker sex. To those who would follow in her tire tracks, she recommended an American car, since they had higher clearance than those of Great Britain and Europe, along with ropes, shovels, spare parts, tire chains, and extra links for chain-driven cars.

Among those already living in the West who heard the call, few were more full of the proper spirit of adventure than Montana resident Kathryn Stephen. Having decided along with old friends Iva and Aunt Isa that a road trip was in order, the three women bought a used Ford and christened it Oliver Twist. On a warm June day in 1922 Oliver was loaded with clothing, fishing tackle, three pie tins, a small ax, twenty feet of rope, a couple of kettles, and a big blue telescope, at which point the women climbed aboard and set off down the Rockies to see the West. In the weeks leading up to the trip a number of friends had all but pleaded with them to enlist the company of a man—"They're so handy for pumping tires," explained one. But they would have none of it.

"Aunt Isa could not run a car at all," writes Kathryn, "I learned after we bought it, and Iva, tho she had driven for several years on the Kansas prairies, boasted no experience on mountain roads." At Monida Pass, in southwest Montana on the Idaho border, the route grew wretched— "smoozy with gumbo mud." Within the hour the three explorers—including Aunt Isa, who was well into her sixties—were down on their knees in the slop putting on chains. When that didn't work they resorted to chopping sagebrush with the hand ax "in a vain attempt to fill up the mud holes that gurgled around our four hubs." After several hours of this torture someone finally came along with a team of horses, hooked up to the car, and pulled it free.

Like most automobiles of that era, the horn on Oliver Twist was driven from the engine, which meant that in low gear at slow speeds there was little in the way of noisemaking power. Desperate for some means of warning oncoming traffic on hairpin turns, the women took to blowing madly on a referee's whistle. The shrill blast of the whistle, though, proved even more nerve-racking than the thought of a collision, so in the end they gave it up, crossed their fingers, and hoped for the best. Flat tires were common; along one stretch the travelers changed nine tires in three days. (Before leaving they'd established a specific protocol for the tire pump, each person limited to no more than thirty strokes in a single turn.) Even with tires full of air the rocks and ruts often forced a snail's pace, which on some days meant average speeds of a paltry five or six miles an hour. Brake linings burned out on mountain roads, backs and shoulders ached from clutching the steering wheel.

By the time these three explorers began their journey, auto camps were sprouting up all along the Rockies, most built by local communities to entice car campers to pitch their tents and spend a few extra dollars at the local grocery, hardware, restaurant, and mechanic. Out-of-staters were thrilled by such facilities; besides amenities like showers, they allowed for the trading of information about everything from road conditions to restaurants. They were decidedly less popular with locals, including Kathryn, Iva, and Aunt Isa. "We had an antipathy to the orthodox camp," writes Kathryn. "They had always seemed so crowded and so— khaki! We objected to being permanently dun and indistinguishable among the dusty mob. We registered only when we needed to wash our clothes or ourselves, or when no more interesting place presented itself." Which wasn't often. Along their route the women slept in a boathouse and on front porches, in haystacks and in a log cabin with a loft filled with pack rats; in canyons, out in the desert, and, at least on one occasion, smack-dab in the middle of the road.

Such travelers almost always wrote kindly of the Rockies, even when they were struggling with blowouts and blizzards. Yet many grew frustrated trying to write descriptions of the sensational attractions they found. Struggling to depict Yellowstone's extraordinary Mammoth Hot Springs in the late 1800s, Horace Edwards finally throws up his hands and turns instead to those around him. "One cannot form any correct impression of this place until he sees it. The girls all clap their hands and say it's splendid, and the old ladies say it's beautiful and go in the tent and take a cup of tea. Laner Williams says it's sublime, but he's in love with Amanda Woodworth and ain't expected to know anything else." Not only that, continues Edwards, pointing out an equally troubling circumstance that was no doubt clouding Laner Williams's judgment: "He is also out of tobacco."

CHAPTER

Preachers with Paintbrushes

Alice's Adventures in the New Wonderland, the Yellowstone National Park
(1885)

As America was increasingly driven by science and industry, those trying
to attract visitors to the Rockies sold the region as a stronghold of imagination and enchantment. This 1885 brochure from the Northern Pacific
Railway builds on Lewis Carroll's popular tale of *Alice's Adventures in
Wonderland*, originally published in 1865.

WHILE ARTISTS WHO TRAVELED WITH men like William Drummond Stewart and Prince Maximilian provided no end of glorious fodder for the American imagination, the Rockies also proved a force of change for the artists themselves. With the exception of that exquisite slice of New England that inspired the famous Hudson River School of art, it's hard to imagine a more important landscape for nineteenth-century painters. By the middle 1800s many of the biggest guns of the art world—men like Thomas Hill, William Keith, Albert Bierstadt, and Thomas Moran—were eagerly making forays westward to the mountains. What they gained there wasn't merely the chance to sketch and paint new, still more outrageous scenery but the opportunity to toss off once and for all a long-standing prejudice of the art world: namely, that it was futile to paint landscapes that had no clear sign of a human presence. This almost fanatical belief, known as the Doctrine of Association, turned on the idea that the only art worth producing was that which had direct ties to a historical past. It would be a long time, argued European critics especially, before Americans would produce any worthwhile landscape art, because in truth the land had little to offer in the way of cultural reference points. (Not that such a perspective was limited to art. In 1857 the editors of *Magazine of Travel* announced that "travels, to be good for anything, must be literary"—a reference to the idea that a proper destination was one with links to antiquity. Or as Thoreau put it, "the partially cultivated country it is which chiefly has inspired, and will continue to inspire, the strains of poets such as compose the mass of any literature.")

Nonsense, said Thomas Cole of Hudson River School fame. The lack of human associations was what was most right about American scenery. While the European landscape had long ago been wiped clean of its primitive characteristics, America's wild lands provoked deeper, more stirring emotions—not because they were free of associations, but because they offered the one association more significant than any other, which was the chance to see God's creation undefiled. Those who would gaze on such scenes, said Cole, were bound to find their mind "cast into the contemplation of eternal things." Not that landscape artists of the Hudson River School weren't happy to portray scenes reflecting the hand of man. Cole's own *The Oxbow*—considered by many to be among the most important paintings of the century—includes the kind of pastoral bliss that was long the ideal in Europe and Great Britain, here represented by an unruffled bend in the Connecticut River, cradled by farmland. Resting in the foreground of that same canvas, though, are remnants of a thunderstorm drifting across a tattered run of unkempt wilderness.

Landscape painters of the day had long been encouraged to think of their work as a sacred duty, their responsibility being to capture from nature essential truths that would help guide people through the important religious and philosophical struggles of their lives. Students of the

Hudson River School regularly found themselves engaged in discussions with teachers about the scripture of art. For his part, Thomas Cole brought a remarkable level of reverence to his frequent sketching trips, often stopping en route to pull out his flute and play a song or two—his way, he explained, of speaking to the landscape. Landscape paintings were understood as narratives, a symbolic rendering of hope and fear, democracy, freedom, and creativity. The stately American elm tree, for example, which shows up on countless canvases of the day, would become the symbol of choice for denoting the promise of freedom in the New World. Likewise, because in England oak trees were used to mark property boundaries, here in America they tended to appear on the canvas broken and decayed, often as charred stumps, thereby sending a clear message about the decadence of a social system favoring the landed gentry.

Nineteenth-century American artists didn't invent such a perspective. They inherited it. "I could not but reflect with pleasure on the situation of these people," wrote Englishman Andrew Burnaby from atop the Blue Ridge in 1760, capturing a sentiment common among many foreign travelers at the time. "They are everywhere surrounded with beautiful prospects, sylvan scenes, lofty mountains, transparent streams, falls of water, rich vallies and majestic woods." Thomas Jefferson took such a sentiment further, assuring readers that visitors to Virginia's Natural Bridge would find it unlikely "for the emotions arising from the sublime to be felt beyond what they are here. The rapture is really indescribable." Meanwhile, six hundred miles to the north one well-traveled Dr. Belnap found himself so overwhelmed by the beauty of the White Mountains that he felt compelled to issue a warning to anyone thinking of venturing there. "Curb the imagination and exercise judgment with mathematical precision, or the temptation to romance will be invincible." Little wonder the Yale class of 1781 was sent into the world with a poetry reading casting nature not as something to be conquered for the glory of God, as many of their forefathers had believed, but in a kindly, even benevolent light. "The bays stretch their arms and mountains lift the skies," gushed the commencement speaker. "And all the majesty of nature smiles."

While patrolling as a soldier in 1790 during the Whiskey Rebellion, Vermont farmer James Elliot topped an unknown summit in Pennsylvania's Blue Mountains. "The sun had risen about an hour before we moved this morning," he writes in his journal. "Began to ascend the mountains and after a fatiguing march of two or three hours reached the summit, where a prospect inexpressibly grand presented itself to our view. To the north, south and west appeared a little world of mountains, arrayed in all the majesty of nature and destitute of a single sign of art or cultivation." Within thirty years all of New England would be on fire with the possibilities of landscape.

Even the fundamentalists would be affected by American nature. A later Puritan colonist, Jonathan Edwards, while still shunning the wilder aspects of the landscape, began writing of the fields, woods, flowers, and birds of New England as fountains of happiness. Through the beauty of nature, he suggested, we would find not evidence of the fall, but rather signposts pointing the way to God. That even a modest relationship to nature could begin to blossom in this group of conservatives, most of whom only meant to survive the physical world long enough to gain the keys to heaven, is strong testimony to how quickly the land was getting under the skin of the newcomers. As noted scholar Perry Miller would later write: "Nature somehow, by a legerdemain that even so highly literate Christians as the editors of *The New York Review* could not quite admit to themselves, had effectually taken the place of the Bible." (Curiously, one of the movements that helped feed a fresh interest in nature among men like Jonathan Edwards was a remarkable infatuation in Europe and England with a new and improved style of botanical garden. Despite a long list of far-flung wonders described during the age of discovery, not a single explorer had found remnants of the actual Garden of Eden, which to many was a tremendous disappointment. Inspired by science's growing fondness for dissecting and cataloging, it seemed the next best thing to actually locating Eden was to gather up scattered pieces of nature from the various corners of the earth and grow them on home soil, thereby fashioning a compendium of creation closely resembling paradise. America, being relatively untouched, was of particular interest. In all it was a magnificent effort, fueled by the thought that such collections were a chance to weave together critical information about the wisdom of God. "If Bibles faile," William Prynne wrote in the 1600s, "each garden will descry the works of God to us." The first such botanical garden sprouted near Venice in 1545, followed by collections in Leyden, Paris, and finally Oxford.)

In the end, reactions to nature in America would go far beyond the genteel flush often associated with the Romantic era. One reason was no doubt the sheer level of wildness found on this side of the Atlantic. Here was a nearly incomprehensible sprawl of uplands and forests and rivers, hundreds of thousands of square miles of it, exploding utterly the frames through which most people had long imagined the natural world. Back in England, Romantic poet William Wordsworth lamented that for tens of thousands of people, a meadow with fat cattle and a heavy crop of corn is worth "all the Alps and Pyrenees in their utmost grandeur and beauty," while his countryman William Gilpin—the same genius who coined the phrase "rain follows the plow"—told readers in 1791 that there were very few people "who do not prefer the busy scenes of cultivation to the greatest of nature's rough productions." Yet residents of the New World were living close to such unkempt lands, day after day, year after year. And while that exposure didn't necessarily make the wilderness home, at the very least it made it part of the neighborhood.

An enticing consequence of this immersion in nature was that certain types of old, pre-Christian earth tales reawakened with a start. What had long been a fondness for such stories in the folk cultures of Europe and Great Britain (albeit largely underground, out of earshot of the church) would here at the edge of the wilderness return to center stage. The vast majority of the world's nature mythology had unfolded along three persistent themes, or story lines. Jonathan Edwards's fondness for seeing beauty in the fields and flowers, and through beauty, the face of God, had been part of European experience five hundred years earlier— floating quietly through the Catholic church in the form of the Rhineland mystic movement, which included Thomas Aquinas and Mechtild of Magdeburg. "A truly wise person," wrote Mechtild, "kneels at the feet of all creatures." In earlier times, and well before Christianity, came the idea that nature's beauty is a dynamic force, powerful enough to prod humans out of hopelessness, toward some greater sense of accord.

The second motif had to do with community in the broadest sense—a knitting together of relationships not just with other people but with the surrounding landscape and the creatures living there. The Greek version of this was called the chain of being, said to link everything from rocks to plants to humans to spirits. A similar notion appeared in Christian circles, in large part thanks to people like twelfth-century abbess Hildegard von Bingen, who delighted in the notion of the universe as one body. The whole penetrates each of its parts, Hildegard surmised, and thereby created a single whole. "I, the fiery life of divine wisdom, I ignite the beauty of the plains, I sparkle the waters, I burn in the sun, and the moon, and the stars."

The final story line, perennial across the ages and a foundation of every religion, concerns the building of links to what mythologists often call transcendent mystery. This refers to how people imagine those parts of creation beyond understanding, building a body of story and symbols meant not to explain, but merely to hint at the essence of things unknown. One way such fascination could be expressed was through a kind of theater of the invisibles, where unseen beings guided, healed, and inspired daily life. This is what underlies the Celtic world of pixies, sprites, and the like— so-called little people—responsible for everything from healing sick animals to causing flowers to bloom in the spring. (Later, as the British Isles became more settled, those same invisibles stepped out of the wild and took up residence in the garden, often as fairies.)

Early traders in northeastern America showed an enormous appetite for this idea of a nature populated with invisibles. French trappers soaked up stories of the "puckwudgies," or "little vanishers," from the Penobscot Indians, as well as the Ho-no-che-no-keh ("invisible agents") of the Iroquois. Before long the exploits of Indian deities were showing up on the other side of the Atlantic, sometimes blended into stories about a popular French fictional character known as "Little Jack." Later, in the early 1800s, one of the most critically acclaimed pieces of literature to appear in America was *The Culprit Fay*, an Arthurian-style story told in verse, filled with beings who seemed half English pixie and half Penobscot puckwudgie. Rational scientific thought aside, this love for the mysterious—particularly in the context of wild places—would continue to thrill Americans well into modern times. Even so cogent a voice as the *New York Times* seemed enamored of the unknown. "There is something romantic," claimed an 1871 editorial about the Rockies, "in the thought that, in spite of the restless activity of our people, and the almost fabulous rapidity of their increase, vast tracts of the national domain yet remain unexplored. As little is known of these regions as of the topography of the sources of the Nile or the interior of Australia. They are enveloped in a certain mystery. . . ."

These perennial drivers of myth—beauty, mystery, and community—were the roots of what American landscape artists kept alive throughout the nineteenth century—first in New England and later in the Rockies. That said, the more time passed, the more they struggled, arguing for such ideas in the face of an increasingly rational, literal world, one driven more and more by science, industry, and wealth. "The wise and the foolish," wrote biologist A. R. Wallace in the middle of the nineteenth century, "the learned and the unlearned, the rich and the poor alike swell with admiration for the inventions and discoveries of our own age, which remind us every hour of our immense superiority over our comparatively ignorant forefathers." Matters of myth and symbolic narrative were increasingly marginalized, presented as fuzzy attempts by second-rate minds to explain what they couldn't understand.

OUTSIDE THE EASTERN CITIES where major exhibitions of Rocky Mountain art took place—nearly always to overwhelming acclaim—much of the public would be exposed to the mountains by way of the illustrations that accompanied a raft of no-nonsense accounts by government explorers. Such efforts exposed a tremendous number of people to artistic glimpses of the Rockies. Official renderings of both the Rocky Mountains and the Sierras amounted to the largest government-based patronage of the arts in American history. Between 1843 and 1863 more than seven hundred prints of various western scenes were released, mostly in book form, to accompany the published reports of various federal surveys and expeditions; as Martha Sandweiss reports, the seven volumes of the Pacific Railroad surveys alone were likely seen by millions. Yet whatever intention an expedition artist may have had to reclaim the sacred (and some were hoping for just that), in this context their work—much of it altered significantly by other artists before publication—seemed mostly intended to, as William Goetzmann describes it, "dramatize the West as the American destiny."

By the final decades of the century, critics were routinely dismissing the idea of painting as narrative, rejecting everything but the most faithful scenic reproductions. Albert Bierstadt—in the 1860s a heroic visionary whose painting *Rocky Mountains, Landers Peak* sold for a record $25,000—was thirty years later being severely criticized by everyone from magazine editors to Mark Twain for being too imaginative. Bierstadt, who understood well the role of art in keeping alive our relationship to the transcendent, complained bitterly, saying he'd never set out to produce a record of the landscape. "I place no value on literal transcripts from nature," he sniffed. "All my tendencies are toward idealization. Topography in art is valueless." Likewise Thomas Moran, only somewhat less inclined toward exaggeration in his paintings of the Rockies than Bierstadt, would spend much of his time scoffing at critics of imaginative art. As Charles Dudley Warner reflected in the *Atlantic* in 1879: "We used to hear, years ago, a great deal about an American school of landscape painting. We don't know what has become of it now. . . ."

It was there, all right, stubbornly blooming as best it could. Given the rapid, even overwhelming loss of wild lands in the East in the middle 1800s, appreciating the American landscape through the beauty and mystery of the Rockies and Sierras was considered by some the last best chance for a nation to save the roots of its identity. "The spirit of our society is to contrive but not to enjoy," wrote Thomas Cole, "toiling to produce more toil—accumulating in order to aggrandize. The pleasures of the imagination, among which the love of scenery holds a conspicuous place, will alone temper the harshness of such a state; and, like the atmosphere that softens the most rugged forms of the landscape, cast a veil of tender beauty over the asperities of life." It's easy to see how such lofty interpretations might lead to some over-the-top art. Yet these same thoughts informed the work of some of the country's most notable writers and philosophers, from Walt Whitman to John Muir.

It's especially interesting how these artists handled the last of those three great mythical motifs: the idea of community. As the nineteenth century wore on, most signs of Western civilization, including humans, began vanishing from the canvas. While in 1855 Hudson River School artist Frederic Church was routinely painting scenes of the Maine outback with pastoral foregrounds, five years later the wilds had all but taken over. Even the magnificent portrait artist Karl Bodmer, known for his highly accurate images of natives along the Missouri River, included in his work few of the tools or decorations those cultures had acquired from the Anglos.

With the passing decades artists would anchor the idea that Americans were increasingly placing themselves outside the sacred circle of nature. This sense of being estranged from the earth remained a cornerstone of our view of wild places right into modern times. The notion that remote lands in the Rockies and elsewhere should be free of humans wasn't based on any historical reality; people had been roaming the western wilderness—and, to no small extent, altering it—for a good ten thousand years. But it's an image that served well these feelings of estrangement, a means of paying homage to what we imagined as a more grounded, integrated time. Beginning with the landscape artists of the mid-nineteenth century, we came to celebrate the Rocky

Mountain wilderness less as an artifact of history than as a metaphor of the garden before the Fall.

The anxiety of such loss led to a strong public interest not just in art but in any sort of story that seemed to feed this lingering affection for the land. When in 1869 Samuel Bowles reported having seen in Colorado something called the Mountain of the Holy Cross, news of the discovery spread like wildfire. While various explorers had searched for the feature in the past—a snow-filled coular on the steep face of a 14,004-foot peak deep in the Sawatch Range, in the obvious shape of an enormous cross—Bowles was among the first to write about it for a popular audience. He no doubt pleased greatly fans of manifest destiny, pronouncing the attraction as being proof of God's blessing on the expanding empire. "It is as if God has set His sign, His seal, His promise there—a beacon upon the very center and height of the Continent to all the people and all its generations." In the general public, though, most people seemed far more intrigued by the simple inscrutability of the place. In no time at all miraculous events were being associated with the mountain, including reports that even on clear days the entire peak would sometimes mysteriously disappear. What's more, the Mountain of the Holy Cross was said to hold great restorative powers, creating what was for decades a kind of wilderness version of Lourdes. Sixty years later, in 1930, an article in the *Denver Post* reported an unusual number of people recently stricken with various illnesses that defied medical science heading for the Sawatch Range.

"They have hope that a sight of the Holy Cross, coupled with firm faith in divine power, will accomplish cures. Certainly such cures have resulted from the pilgrimages of the last two years."

William Henry Jackson photographed the Holy Cross while rambling the Rockies with Ferdinand Hayden's survey team in 1873. (Due to changing snow conditions the cross was more visible in some seasons than in others; Jackson later doctored the image in the darkroom to give the feature greater prominence.) Two years later it was Thomas Moran's turn. Images from both artists were exhibited at the Centennial Exposition in 1876 to considerable acclaim. In 1929 President Herbert Hoover designated the peak a national monument, though the action was later revoked, in 1950, in part because severe erosion had compromised the right arm of the cross.

IN AMERICA, with glorious dreams come exceptional chances for profit. No industry understood this better than the railroads. Of their various marketing efforts, one of the most steadfast—lasting some fifty years—was an old, familiar patriotic call to "See America First," America in this case being the national parks and dude ranches of the West. The master of that particular lure was Yale-educated Louis Warren Hill, president of the Great Northern Railway and "godfather" of Glacier National Park. (An enthusiastic fan of the park's mountain goats, it was Hill who came up with the idea of using that animal as the logo for the railroad, thereby launching what was arguably one of the most recognizable advertising trademarks of the twentieth century.) Hill had grown so infatuated with the rugged mountain scenery of Glacier that shortly after the park's creation in 1910 he retired from the railroad to devote his every waking hour to bringing in visitors. "The work is so important," he once told his family, "that I am loath to entrust the development to anyone but myself." While some have criticized the relationship between railroads and national parks as crass commercialism—and at times it was exactly that—the Great Northern defended its actions by pointing to the fact that the federal government was completely unwilling to provide even the most rudimentary facilities for park visitors. Hill spent six frenetic years laying out networks of scenic trails and tent camps throughout Glacier, not to mention choosing locations for the magnificent stone and timber lodges built with railroad money, still standing today.

Like other railroad magnates of the day, Hill was well aware of the incredible role landscape art had played in igniting dreams of the Rockies. His advertising efforts included hiring painters like Winold Reiss and John Fery, whose work showed up in everything from art museums to magazines, wall calendars to decks of playing cards. In the years 1910 to 1913 Fery alone completed some 350 paintings for the Great Northern Railway—focusing not just on Glacier but on Yellowstone too—most of them loose and lovely renditions of high mountain peaks, streams, lakes, and wildlife. Some of the works were enormous, measuring over sixty square feet. For his efforts Fery received on average about thirty dollars per painting.

More often than not such art was linked to advertising narrative, some of it by today's standards fairly shameless. In 1885, for example, admen at the Northern Pacific Railway created a long-winded brochure called *Alice's Adventures in the New Wonderland: The Yellowstone National Park.* The cover features a showy painting of a young, somewhat buxom Alice dressed in Victorian clothing and holding a pair of binoculars, with a silk-ribboned hat around her neck and long white gloves, standing against a rugged, rocky mountainscape dappled with pines. Inside is an extremely long letter by Alice to her cousin Edith, in which she recounts her trip by train from St. Paul, Minnesota, to the nation's first national park. It's a tome that even cousin Edith would've been forced to take in rounds. In part it reads:

My Dearest Edith:

When Mr. Carroll wrote that funny book about one of my childish dreams, I little thought the time would ever come when I should sit down and describe scenes and incidents in my actual experience every bit as strange and bewildering. . . . Well, here I am (in Wonderland), rubbing my eyes every day, to be sure that I am not either in a dream or in a new world. . . . But besides the Rocky mountains and a

waterfall—and a big one, too, twice as high as Niagara—
there is the grandest old lot of geysers and boiling springs in
the world, and a river shut in for several miles of its course
by mountains rising hundreds of feet above it, what they call
a canon (pronounced canyon), the walls of which are of such
glowing colors that papa said he could compare it to nothing
but the most gorgeous sunset he had ever seen. . . .

And now I am going to tell you something that you will
scarcely believe. There was a gentleman fishing in the Gard-
ner River, where the hot water flows into it, and after catching a trout, he would, without unhooking it, swing his line
over into the hot water, and in almost as short a time as it
takes to tell it, the fish would be cooked and ready for the
table. What do you think of that? Was there ever anything
more wonderful in a child's dream than the fact of a cold
river and a hot one running side by side and the angler cooking in the one stream the produce of the other. Tell me, is
this not Wonderland? . . .

"And now, dear Edith, do you not think that this region
is rightly named The Wonderland? The Wonderland of the
World? It has been a new experience, an epoch in my life,
and I cannot wish you a better wish than that you may soon
have the good fortune to tread the mysterious soil and gaze
upon the matchless scenes of this new wonderland.

Your affectionate cousin,
Alice

Forty years later the creative team at Great Northern were still at it, coming up with equally inspired copy, including a splashy, art-filled advertisement that ran off and on for years in the *New Yorker* and *Time* magazines. After waxing on about the glories of the Glacier landscape, the final line of the ad attempts to snare both sportsmen and gourmets: "I'll show you broiled trout," it reads, "that would tempt Mahatma Gandhi."

While narrative art and illustration would eventually fall out of favor in much of the country, replaced by photography, it continued to be a driving force in the Rocky Mountain West. Illustrations for railroad brochures sparked wonder and enchantment. Other, equally striking images were routinely tossed across the pages of leading magazines to accompany adventure tales, focusing on manly dangers like grizzlies and mountain lions and wolves. Meanwhile narrative painters like Frederic Remington, Charlie Russell, and Henry Farny spent much of their effort on what was by the turn of the century pure nostalgia: Indians on the move, such as in Farny's magnificent *Indian Marauding Party Fording the Stream,* or *On the Trail in Winter;* adventure and early exploration, such as in Russell's *Lewis and Clark Meeting the Flatheads at Ross' Hole;* or the battle with natives for control of the land, as in Remington's *Fight for the Stolen Herd.*

At the same time landscape artists of the Rockies were keeping alive the idea of wild nature as a source of beauty, community, and mystery, they continued to also think of such places as equalizers, level playing fields where privilege

meant nothing—where democracy seemed to have an especially good chance of flowering. Beyond that, to many of
these same artists the western wilds were considered an outstanding source of physical and mental challenge—a place to
lessen the "softening" influences of civilization, to shore up
the toughness and resourcefulness in which Americans took
such enormous pride. "Here the forms are nearly beyond
comprehension," wrote Clarence Dutton, "the colours rude,
glaring, uncompromising; the effect is inhuman, overpower-
ing; man is crushed and humiliated." Exactly the kind of
place that appealed to the rough-and-ready.

Images of beauty and melancholy, with a dose of danger and hardship. Such was the artistic mix that became
entrenched in the late nineteenth century, and would persist
for the next hundred years. It was thanks in great part to
American landscape artists that the Rockies were thus destined to evolve not simply as a unique place on the continent
but also as a collection of things hoped for and lost. The
province of dreams.

CHAPTER 7

A Monaco Gambling Room in a Colorado Spruce Clearing

***Buffalo Bill Cody's Wild West Show Brochure* (1911)**
Destined to become the most recognizable human on earth, Buffalo Bill
Cody proved a master at exploiting a worldwide melancholy for the pass-
ing of the frontier West.

L ONG BEFORE AMERICANS MET THE ROCKY Mountains, the world had been overflowing with mythical accounts of gold hidden in remote nooks and vales of the high country. But whereas in many societies those stories were understood as allegories for spiritual development, in California and the Rockies the tales were taken literally. Beyond the exploits of the Spanish explorer Alvarado, who had been led out of New Mexico on that wild-goose chase to find the rich lands of Quivira, the Spanish continued to roam the southern portions of the range for decades, on fire with hope. One of the earliest legends of that region turns on the story of an army regiment in the New Mexico high country, in the company of priests, stumbling across a fabulous vein of gold. Forcing local Indians to dig it out, the men then moved south over Cuchara Pass, planning to then head west across the Sangre de Cristo Range. Instead they found hostile natives waiting, who wasted no time killing the entire lot. To this day the river is known as the Animas, short for Río de las Animas Perdido en Purgatorio, or the River of Lost Souls in Purgatory. Centuries later, in 1859, the discovery of gold in Colorado, followed by subsequent discoveries in Idaho and Montana, sparked the fever all over again, enticing thousands of Americans who imagined riches waiting for anyone who heard the call.

In the opening rounds of the Colorado gold rush, between roughly 1859 and 1867, the mines yielded more than a million and a quarter ounces of gold. And that was just the beginning. The Cripple Creek mining district, discovered in 1891, would in its first two years produce $3 million worth of ore; by the end of the rush that figure had swelled to more than $430 million, making this the fourth-largest gold-producing region in the world. Since 1859 Colorado mines have yielded roughly forty-five million ounces of gold, not to mention fabulous amounts of silver and other precious metals. The largest silver nugget in the world was found near Aspen in 1894, weighing in at a staggering 1,840 pounds.

Beyond big payoffs and even more stellar bankruptcies, mining affected everything from the fate of native cultures to the establishment of territories. One of Abraham Lincoln's constant worries during the Civil War was the inability of the Washington territorial government to control distant gold mines on the west side of the Rockies, near present-day Oro Fino (literally "fine gold" in Italian), Idaho. Lincoln feared that without protection the wealth from those mines might be diverted out of the territory to the South, and used to fund the Confederate cause. In 1863 he moved to partition off the area surrounding the gold fields, combining it with part of Dakota Territory and calling it Idaho—complete with a staff of watchful territorial legislators in the recently chosen capital of Lewiston, a stone's throw from the mines. Gold-mining activity, though, has a habit of changing faster than mountain weather. Not long after Lincoln's move the miners split from Oro Fino to work rich new diggings two hundred miles to the southeast, near the town of Bannack. (Discovered in 1862 by a party of lost miners from Colorado, the Bannack diggings had yielded almost overnight a murderous town of about two thousand, run by road agents and desperadoes.) But by the following year that party had fizzled, too, sending miners looking for still more possibilities at Virginia City. When Virginia City was platted in June of 1863, it was part of Idaho Territory, just as Bannack had been. Thanks to another push from Lincoln, though, barely a year passed before Virginia City became part of yet another new territory, this one called Montana, with yet another set of government officials established at the territorial capital to keep close watch on the gold.

While in their day trappers had greatly diminished their essential resource, wiping beaver out altogether in some watersheds, compared to the miners they were old ladies with butterfly nets. The mere rumor of gold, every bit as much as the actual discovery, sparked a kind of chaos in the high country not seen before or since. Almost overnight quiet roads through remote parts of Colorado and Montana were choked with cursing teamsters plodding through ankle-deep mud, wagons piled high with flour and cornmeal and whiskey and railroad iron, drivers laying the whips without mercy to their horses and mules. Would-be prospectors and their wives and children headed up-country as well—hundreds, sometimes thousands at a time. Great flocks of crows and ravens hugged the roads, scattering before each passing group and then settling again, feeding on grain spilled from the wagons. Many prospectors traveled on foot, pickax in hand and no more than what they could carry either on their backs or on a lone pack mule; others went with small box wagons crammed with cooking stoves and cradles and bedsteads and iron pots. Some were fresh and full of hope. For others it was simply a forced march from another mine, often a hundred or more miles away, a wave of humanity washed down one mountain and up the next by yet another boom gone bust.

Entire mountainsides stood stripped of timber—sometimes from fires, more often harvested for woodstoves and reduction furnaces and for shoring up the mines. In spring and summer mud spilled across the exposed slopes in great torrents, belching into streams that were mere shadows of their former selves—dredged, dug into gullies and side channels to feed rickety lines of sluice boxes. The remaining flow, grimy and brown, was then diverted into small ditches that carried it as drinking and cooking water to strings of makeshift hovels squatting nearby. In towns where things hadn't gone as well as hoped—and those were the majority—the ground remained for years littered with dilapidated shacks and dead chickens and cats, piles of tin cans and scattered pieces of cloth and rags and rotting straw. Walking through such a sight in the town of Fair Play, the normally delighted journalist Helen Hunt seems about to fall to her knees under the weight of the gloom. "It was a spot for despair," she said, "for murders, for suicides."

Successful mining camps, on the other hand, may have been nearly as dingy, but at the same time were electrified with activity. "A Monaco gambling room emptied into a Colorado spruce clearing," as Helen Hunt described Leadville. In small openings in the woods around the towns, reduction furnaces spewed fire and smoke into the cool, thin air; beside them, row after row of bins stuffed with ore from the surrounding mines. Streams of waste material ejected from the furnaces went into iron buckets fastened to two-wheeled carts, then rolled away and dumped in piles on the ground. Elsewhere pairs of men could be seen hovering over deep cavities in the earth, straining at the handles of wooden cranks, hauling up ore buckets shoveled full by unseen partners sweating through the day some twelve or fifteen feet below. The outskirts of such camps were a mix of tepees, tents, and cabins plunked down in a hurry over loose tosses of stumps, the chimneys often made from stray pieces of stovepipe, even flowerpots. As often as not there was a single main street lined with wood-frame buildings, housing livery stables and hotels, dance halls and wash houses and bakeries and banks. And always in the streets, knots of men talking and gesturing—restless, on the edge of something big. "So many men getting rich of a sudden," writes Helen Hunt; "so many men getting poor; crowds pouring in to snatch at chances."

In most districts, Sunday was reserved if not exactly for a day of rest, then one of debauchery. Miners drifted down from the hills by the hundreds to lay down much of their week's earnings in dance houses, brothels, and saloons, every one of which was doing its level best to make the men feel welcome. It was a worthwhile effort, considering that for many businesses the miners and their money were their only real means of support. The typical miner is a man of low tastes, reported one writer in the *Atlantic Monthly*. "He considers Colt, with his revolvers, a broader philanthropist than Raikes with his Sunday schools. But he is frank and open, generous and confiding, honorable and honest, scorning anything mean and cowardly." That said, the writer continued, the miner was also a slow learner, unable to profit from unwise decisions of the past, blowing his wad in one place and then hitting the trail when the party was over. "The same bacchanalian orgies follow the next full purse."

This "pouring in to snatch at chances," as Helen Hunt put it, led to a mass obliteration of the native way of life. Existing treaties proved not worth the paper they were written on, and as the years passed Indians up and down the mountains were huddled onto smaller and smaller reservations. Those unwilling to cooperate often retreated to the safety of the mountains, though their days too were numbered. In Colorado, when miners illegally stormed Ute territory in the San Juan Mountains in the early 1860s, a new agreement was hammered out—the Kit Carson Treaty, named for the old trapper who negotiated between the government and the brilliant, multilingual Chief Ouray—but because of gold fever, by 1879 it too was in shambles. Thus four centuries after the Ute arrived in Colorado (at the time they were the longest-living permanent residents by some 250 years), a century after they pulled Spanish explorer Silvestre Velez de Escalante's *cajones* out of the fire by saving his party from death by thirst, no less a bastion of journalism than *Harper's Weekly* declared, "The Utes must go!" And go they did. But not without some inspired maneuvering through the high country, evading capture time and again, holding out to become the last American tribe to pass into government control.

While it was the government that often played the heavy, sending in troops to rout the Indians whenever necessary, in truth it seems unlikely political leaders would've been able to contain the gold rush frenzy even if they'd wanted to. Writing of the Bannack Indians, formerly from the lands that became gold fields near Virginia City, Montana, an unnamed writer for the *Atlantic Monthly* called them the bravest, the proudest, and the noblest-looking Indians of the mountains. Yet the rush to gold had proved a striking illustration of the fact that "every step of the white man's progress has been a step of the red man's decay. And now this tribe, once so war-like, is a nation of spiritless beggars, crouching near the white settlements for protection from their old foes, over whom in times past they were easy victors."

On it went, from Colorado to Montana to New Mexico and back again, a belching cloud of wandering nomadic miners. Though the vast majority never found anything close to the mother lode—indeed they were sometimes lucky to make a day's wage—others made fortunes and promptly blew them, while still others turned out to be good boys who filled their saddlebags and headed for home. More than a few left promising digs simply for the chance to keep wandering. In a remarkable episode in 1887, one unlucky fellow by the name of Tom Groves got rich one day and lost it the next without ever spending a cent. Groves uncovered an enormous nugget of gold in the mountains of Colorado, which he quietly wrapped in a blanket and carried to the home of the local assayer. Christened "Tom's Baby," the nugget weighed a whopping thirteen pounds seven ounces. Having made arrangements to ship his treasure to the big city for safekeeping, Grove loaded it on a train bound for Denver, where it promptly disappeared; it remained missing for eighty-five years—where it was is still anyone's guess— finally showing up again in a Federal Reserve vault in 1972, long after Tom was dead and gone.

Many young men who came to the camps spent a fair amount of their time writing in journals, ruminating, trying to pull some sense out of the chaos going on all around them. Joseph Warren Arnold, for example, writes on July 12, 1864:

> I today went down the gulch looking for work. At . . . the mines saw a couple of Dutchmen shoveling methodically into a string of sluices and smoking clay pipes, thinking contentedly of the time when they would return to Faderland— Caterina—sourkraut—and lager beer. Further down the gulch I saw a . . . boy with his partner from ould Ireland taking a wee drap of the craythur just to take off the bad taste of

the water. Bad luck to it preparatory to the days of labor. Further down I found a company of Americans unshaven and unshorn, rough spoken and rougher clad, digging away with philosophical indifference and hoping for success, yet meeting ill luck with grim patience. They are old miners and have learned to meet misfortune with steady front. Higher up and lower down can be found similar companies and be heard the same sounds. The primeval silence of former times has given away to the sounds of human industry, the merry flutter of wheels, the splashing creaking of pumps and all the bustle and activity of a mining life. I found no work. They said I was a tenderfoot and couldn't stand it, so I returned to our cabin, sat down, began to think of hard times and the coming winter.

ONE PERCEPTION THAT STUCK with many who stayed on in the Rockies past the mining era was a striking sense of boom and catastrophic bust—a perspective brought on by a series of depression-level losses, often only seasons apart. Arguably, the rags-to-riches-to-rags story was played out with as much intensity in the gold- and silver-bearing regions of the Rockies as anywhere in the country; it fed unreasonable hope, and at the same time a kind of supreme fatalism which bordered on pathos. The result was a joyous, even reckless kind of living for the present, investing with abandon in any happy diversion that presented itself. Future concerns, be they of health or heaven, were of little importance. "When a whole community regards life as a picnic," Rollin Lynde Hartt had written of the Montana mining scene, "the parson can be dispensed with." Save for a very few, "nobody expects to stay in Montana—just hang out long enough to get rich and then get away." One day, however, says Hartt, all that will have to change. "Montana needs women. Montana needs homes. Montana needs to acquire the art of staying put."

The boom-and-bust cycles of extractive industry also helped create a brand of boosterism that at times bordered on the lunatic. When in 1967 *Redbook* had the audacity to assign the name "Big Sky Country" to Arizona, California, Nevada, New Mexico, and Utah, Montana tourism promoters went ballistic. The mayor of Billings wrote a letter to the magazine's editor, passing himself off as an Indian leader known as "Chief of the Big Sky Country." He warns that scalping parties were being formed to deal with *Redbook*'s plagiarism and theft. "[A. B.] Guthrie gave this name—The Big Sky Country—to our Montana land, it was ours for keeps, and we have no intention of letting anyone steal it. I might also advise you," he goes on to say, "that only four times has the American Army ever been truly licked, and all four times it was Montanans who administered that threshing—at the Big Hole, the Rosebud, the Fetterman Massacre, and the Custer-Sitting Bull Battle. And as Custer can attest—when we lick 'em, they stay licked. So if you think we will take this sneaking thievery lying down, you underestimate the courage of my fellow tribesmen."

Even the most raucous days of the gold rush found small groups of people fiercely devoted to stabilizing the region, bending over backward to convince families back east that they should make the Rockies home. In 1877 enthusiastic boosters of Colorado Territory published a small booklet typical of the era called *Resources and Advantages of Colorado.* The advantages, say the authors, are incredible. For one thing, in this golden land it takes but a modest amount of honest labor to coax forth "gigantic crops." What's more, horses, cattle, and sheep live so easily year-round in the lower elevations that they "never have to be fed." As for the high mountain valleys, where winter may settle in seven or even eight months, readers can rest assured that the climate is nonetheless delightful, that these uplands are destined to become "one of the great dairy districts of the United States."

At the same time, the pamphlet faces head-on a great source of irritation among many westerners at the time, which was that educated easterners were constantly denigrating residents of the Rockies as ignorant ruffians and yahoos. In truth many easterners really did feel that way, in part because they'd been well schooled in exactly that view by decades of popular fiction. What's more, it was a long time before the mountain states produced much in the way of notable writers and artists, which to some indicated a serious lack of sophistication. Traveling through Leadville, Oscar Wilde writes tongue in cheek of a former miner he met who'd struck it rich, and with his newfound wealth decided to become a patron of the arts. Wilde explains how at one point the man sued the railroad for damages when a plaster cast of Venus of Milo, imported from Paris, was delivered minus the arms. More surprising still, adds Wilde, "he gained his case and the damages." The boosters were not amused. "While such people universally underrate the intelligence of both our professional men and our citizens," they snuffled, "in truth there's a higher grade of intelligence in Colorado than anywhere in the old settled states. . . . He who comes amongst us appears to catch the inspiration of his surroundings, and is filled with loftier aims and a nobler ambition than that which moved him in the regions from whence he has come."

If potential newcomers to the Rockies from the East and Midwest took promises of carefree cattle and superintelligent citizens with a grain of salt, few would've been so quick to dismiss another claim made in *Resources and Advantages of Colorado*, which was the promise of good health. Any person with a fair constitution who settles in any portion of Colorado, wrote Dr. F. J. Bancroft of Denver, "stands a better chance of enjoying a healthful life, and of finally attaining the full period allotted to man—three score years and ten—than in any other part of the Union." Should you doubt the healthfulness of the Rockies, suggests Bancroft, you need only consider an 1886 health report on the city of Denver, "which shows the death ratio of that place to be only ten to every one thousand inhabitants, a fact unequalled in any other city in the Union."

Late nineteenth-century physician-boosters like Bancroft (and there were literally hundreds of them scattered up and down the Rockies) were still leaning on a popular if somewhat outdated notion that disease was caused not by germs, but by miasma—a kind of invisible, dynamic fog thought to permeate every living creature. Miasma, it was believed, cut the flow of the vital force streaming through the body, thereby diminishing life-preserving energy. For much of the century one specific type of miasma—psora, from the Hebrew and Greek words for groove—was thought to be responsible for nearly all the chronic illnesses known to man.

These same physicians also traded on a theory popular since the days of Hippocrates, which said that nature was an outward reflection of the inner world, affected by similar forces and healed by similar cures. That "invisible fog" of the body, for example, showed up outwardly as a literal fog on the landscape, something to be avoided at all costs. While it was okay to live on lands that were moist, under no circumstances should they be swampy, since this could easily lead to malaria. In the same way a doctor in the middle of the century would let blood from a sick person, so too could you release the potential for a dangerous miasma by draining swamps and cutting vegetation. Breezy conditions were fine, windy ones were not. Flowing water was good, but well water was potentially disastrous. Miasma was also associated with plant and animal decay. Thus while an Indian of the 1870s stumbling across a prairie full of casually slaughtered buffalo might find it a tragic waste, many Anglos coming across the same scene would likely have had as their first thought the potential such carnage had as a breeding ground for deadly illness. Given the lingering popularity of such ideas, few Americans would have questioned the notion that the climate of the Rockies was likely to be healthier than that of a lot of other places.

Miasma, said some experts, were also increasingly taking hold in large towns and cities of the East and Midwest, as the air became more polluted from smokestack industries. Such pollution had already been linked to one of the most dreaded diseases of the day, tuberculosis, which at the time was defined as an inability to get the proper amount of oxygen into the lungs. Once again, it was the Rockies to the rescue. At high elevations, explained Dr. Bancroft, one has to consciously expand the chest to the fullest to secure sufficient oxygen, thereby exercising the lungs and guarding against lung-related illness. "With these qualities in such a climate, its bright days inducing out-door sports, and its cold nights for refreshing slumber, one can easily understand that even a short residence therein would cause the narrow in chest to become broad, the relaxed in muscle to grow strong, the thin in flesh to gain in weight."

Finally, in the latter part of the century there was increasing public dissatisfaction with traditional medicine. Pharmaceuticals were increasingly suspect. People were irritated with what they considered a tendency in doctors to throw up their hands over diseases for which there seemed to be no cure. As a result, more and more people sought holistic cures, the most common being a simple formula of fresh air and vigorous exercise. Doctors eventually climbed on board, too, prescribing climate-related remedies for illnesses like consumption, tuberculosis, and various types of fever; in time dry air and wholesome atmosphere were widely recognized conditions for health, fully acknowledged by most physicians. Little wonder that according to territorial surveys, in the 1880s one-third of immigrants to Colorado were coming either for the chance to cure existing ailments or to be in a land where many of the most dreaded diseases were all but unknown.

IN THE FINAL DECADE of the nineteenth century, there came a startling announcement: according to settlement figures compiled by the Census Bureau in 1890—basically, an appraisal of the number of residents per square mile—the frontier West was officially closed. The news caused great anxiety among countless Americans. If the finest qualities of our people were products of wilderness, after all, then who would we be when the wilderness was gone? It was a question at the heart of a famous thesis offered by historian Frederick Jackson Turner—some say the most famous essay in American history—claiming that our struggle with the wild frontier was the single most important factor in shaping national identity. "American democracy was born of no theorist's dream," Turner said in what would become the most frequently quoted comment of his life. "It was not carried in the *Susan Constant* to Virginia, nor in the *Mayflower* to Plymouth. It came out of the American forest, and it gained a new strength each time it touched a new frontier."

The frontier was thought of as much more than just a place where people could homestead on free land. In the years following the announcement by the Census Bureau, Henry George's *Progress and Poverty*—already one of the best-selling books of the century thanks to its tirades against the robber barons—enjoyed a new burst of sales, this time because of what it had to say about our relationship to public lands. "The free, independent spirit, the energy and hopefulness that have marked our people are not causes, but results," wrote George. "They have sprung from unfenced land. Public domain has given a consciousness of freedom even to the dweller in crowded cities, and has been a wellspring of hope even to those who have never thought of taking refuge upon it."

Such hope was further stoked by a growing perception that much of the promise of the Industrial Revolution had withered on the vine. People in cities across the country watched with mounting frustration as the length of the workweek grew while wages plummeted. In rural areas agricultural wealth was becoming ever more concentrated, forcing thousands of independent farmers to take jobs as tenants or sharecroppers on corporate farms. Health was at its lowest point in decades, driven by work-related accidents, by massive outbreaks of emphysema and tuberculosis. The most comprehensive social study of the day concluded that some ten million people, or roughly 15 percent of the population, were so poor they couldn't afford food and clothing—this, even though fully 20 percent of all children were working twelve- to fourteen-hour days in mills, mines, and factories. Nervous disorders from insomnia to high blood pressure were growing at terrifying rates. All this despite assurances by pundits decades earlier that science and technology was on the verge of all but ending human suffering.

Naturalist Ernest Thompson Seton added his two cents in the May 1900 issue of *Century Magazine,* as usual plucking his metaphors from the animal kingdom—this time from monkeys at the Washington Zoo. Until recently, he explained, monkeys in even the best zoological parks were routinely afflicted with coughs, colds, and lung diseases—illnesses that tended to spread rapidly, resulting in massive die-offs of captive animals. It was a dreadful situation, Seton assured readers, until an unnamed European zookeeper decided to discard the normal crowded hothouse environment typically used for monkeys, giving them instead regular exposure to sun, fresh air, and exercise. Illness and death rates fell off sharply. The lower animals are like ourselves, Seton concluded. "To keep them in health we must give some thought to their happiness, and in aiming at both we must accept the ordinary principles obtained from study of ourselves."

Meanwhile Dr. A. E. MacDonald of the Manhattan State Hospital East mental institution was in 1902 making similar discoveries on the human side of the fence. Struggling to prevent an outbreak of tuberculosis, in early summer MacDonald isolated a large number of severely disturbed patients by erecting tents out on the lawns along the East River. (MacDonald shared a then common assumption that mentally ill people were particularly susceptible to tuberculosis.) To his amazement, patients who had been hopelessly bedridden for years were suddenly out walking barefoot in the grass, standing on the banks of the river waving at passing boats. Incontinence dropped, appetites improved, medications were reduced. In a number of cases people thought to have no chance of ever leaving the institution were by the end of the summer being sent home with family members. The following year other doctors at the institution gave the open-air life a try, with equally impressive results. It proved the beginning of an enormously popular treatment regimen known in mental health circles as tent therapy, employed by institutions across the country for the next twenty years. Alas, like many other breakthroughs, tent therapy was a victim of its own success; by the 1920s a growing number of canvas shelters were stuffed to the brim with patients, essentially mimicking the same crowded, unhealthy conditions the movement was meant to overcome.

By 1910 the *Boy Scout Handbook* was outselling every other book except the Bible. There was talk at many of the nation's best universities about starting colleges dedicated to the study and preservation of wilderness. In the summer of 1913 a part-time artist by the name of Joe Knowles stood on

the shores of Maine's King & Bartlett Lake amidst a bewildered group of reporters, stripped down to something close
to a G-string, and walked off into the woods to live as a wild
man for sixty days—just to prove, he explained, that Americans still had sap in their veins. When Knowles finally left
the woods and returned to Massachusetts, some two hundred thousand people were waiting to get a look at him. He
toured vaudeville for two years with top billing, while the
book of his experience—*Alone in the Wilderness*—sold more
than 150,000 copies.

   In the midst of all this Americans found themselves in
a headlong rush to embrace the mythical West—cowboys to
Indians, wild animals to national parks. Of all the entrepreneurs who scrambled to meet that need, no one proved
better at it than that quintessential showman, Buffalo Bill
Cody. Cody's Wild West Show was for thirty years an astonishing success, touring not just the United States but palaces
and other venues across England and Europe. His was an
extravaganza of western fantasy, wrapped in studded saddles
and flashy buckskins, hand-delivered by an entourage of
more than six hundred vaqueros, Indians, cowboys, and
roughriders—not to mention a number of celebrities, from
Annie Oakley to Sitting Bull. Moving the show from city to
city required more than fifty railroad boxcars. ("The Indians
who are with me," Buffalo Bill explained to a writer in Flo-
rence, "are all prisoners of the government of the United
States, and entrusted to me, under my supervision.") For
their part, most of these Indians felt far safer with Cody

than they felt in the hands of the American government. By 1913 fifty million people had seen the Wild West Show— some, like Queen Victoria, several times—making Buffalo Bill Cody hands down the most recognized human being on earth. By some estimates he pulled down roughly a billion words of copy from writers around the world, his antics showing up in magazines and pulp fiction by the ton. When the old showman passed away in 1917, more than twenty-five thousand people turned out in Colorado for the funeral procession.

One of the dignitaries most often celebrated in Buffalo Bill's show, Teddy Roosevelt, was himself struck with a profound sadness about the passing of the frontier—a notion he sometimes fought off with soothing thoughts about yet undiscovered nooks and crannies in the Rockies. Here and there, he wrote in *Ranch Life and the Hunting Trail,* "these restless wanderers of the untrodden wilderness still linger, in wooded fastnesses so inaccessible that the miners have not yet explored them, in mountain valleys so far off that no ranchman has yet driven his herds thither." Frederic Remington had similar longings for the old Rockies, and he was only too happy to lambaste the culture that had nearly extinguished their best qualities. "The Americans have gashed this country up so horribly with their axes, hammers, scrapers, and plows that I always like to see a place which they have overlooked; some place before they arrive with their heavy-handed God of Progress."

By late in the twentieth century tourism was the third

most important economic force in the Rocky Mountains—
one day to be first. For all its benefits, here was an industry
often powered less by the visions of local citizens than by
what developers imagined those from other parts of the
country most wanted to experience. This would prove a
long-standing source of irritation for residents: on the one
hand they desperately needed tourism to survive, but at the
same time many had a fervent wish that the visitors would
either get real or go away.

The fact that western tourist economies were so incredibly ripe with potential had to do with two distinct kinds of
passion for nature flooding through America at the time.
The first saw nature as a rugged challenge—a view flourishing in literally hundreds of hunting and other adventure stories in the popular press. In the waning decades of the
frontier the pages of national magazines were filled with an
endless string of these adventure tales, all turning on manly,
heroic pursuits. From a point shortly after the Civil War,
publications like *Harper's*, *Atlantic Monthly*, and *Scribner's*
seemed locked in a fierce competition to outdo one another
with rugged tales of mountain adventure. If the time had
passed for strutting our stuff by acting out God's will
through manifest destiny, then we could still keep our wits
sharp by going face-to-face with the dangers of the wild.
While such accounts were often respectful of the wild (at a
minimum, they confessed a desire that wild places would
forever be a part of the American landscape), it was the kind
of respect one carries into battle against a worthy opponent.

So enamored of this perspective were some travelers that anything not properly daunting or belligerent was a letdown. Writing about the Colorado high country for *Harper's* in 1872, hunter Colvan Verplanck expresses great disappointment at finding out that the mighty grizzly actually spends much of its time dining on lowly grasshoppers—an unfortunate habit that caused the creature to "dwindle in our estimation." In the end, though, Verplanck comforts himself with the thought that "even this is but another example of the great law of nature, the strong preying upon the weak." Later on, on horseback near timberline, he describes the forest reaching forward in short strips "like courageous, undaunted squads of infantry pressing onward eagerly before their comrades upon the foe. How wonderful a war between natural forces—how obstinate the contest where they meet!" He slips finally into gibberish as he tries to describe the emotional effect of this strange and exciting world (and in the process gives a whole new spin to elk hunting): "The sportsman looks to his rifle as he sees the monstrous tracks of the cinnamon grizzly, and by the campfire listens with surprise to stories of adventures with mountain lions, of hand-to-hand encounters with elk. . . ."

At the same time, however, another mythic stream was building—one strikingly different from that which saw nature as a stage for heroic struggle. These were tales that painted the wild as munificent, a source of solace and entertainment, health and inspiration. While it was hardly a new perspective—landscape artists had been touting such values for over fifty years—by the end of the century it had tremendous power for the public at large. To some degree this was due to the fact that the alternative story line, the survival of the fittest, seemed increasingly to have been hijacked by wealthy men sitting on top of the capitalist heap. Social Darwinism, the movers and shakers liked to call it. (In truth Darwin had little to do with it. Not only did his theory of natural selection spin on pure chance, but never for a moment had he perceived it as a tool for plotting human morals or social behavior.) Even so, to be able to write off the destruction of Native Americans as the natural way of things, to dismiss growing poverty and disease in urban regions as a failure of motivation, presented a grand piece of pseudoscience to have in your pocket. Such men were hardly ignorant of the fact that America had pinned much of its worldview, from religion to patriotism, on the dynamics of nature. What could be better than nature herself endorsing the idea that those in control were meant to be there?

It's difficult to overestimate the uneasiness surrounding such blustery attitudes—what was often described as a tyranny of the rich. "Enterprise used to mean a sort of actualized epic poetry," wrote Rollin Lynde Hartt. "Now it means a dull materialism." Some writers went so far as to argue that while America had long prided itself on shunning inherited titles and aristocracy, the very absence of those artificial distinctions had placed undue significance on the one social marker that did exist, which was personal wealth. As wonderful as equality of opportunity was, Charles Dudley Warner wrote in 1879, it could also lead to discontent with any position in life except the most conspicuous. "And so the whole community is on the march to get into what is called society, or to get the supposed luxuries and enjoyments of society, through the only gates open to all, that is, by means of money." This in turn, Warner suggested, created some uniquely American behaviors: a willingness to take on heavy debt for the sake of luxury; a cultural personality that seemed at times obsessively industrious; and, last but not least, young people who were more concerned with the opportunity for high-profile careers than with the training necessary to excel in such stations—to get something, as Warner put it, rather than to be something.

According to this train of thought, the real danger of American-style equality was that it could lead to an excessive hunger for the one thing that might destroy equality altogether. When fairly distributed, wealth was a tremendous strength; if not, it was a poison. While leading pundits in the final decades of the century were quick to praise America's accomplishments, they also brought attention to the fact that the country's first hundred years had been remarkably destructive. Millions of acres of forest had been destroyed. Countless lakes and rivers were polluted. Prominent corporate empires, from cotton to railroads, had been built on the backs of slaves, as well as the much abused Chinese. The solution, Warner argued, was simplicity—"making the journey of this life with just baggage enough." And when it came to figuring out what was just enough, there had in America never been a better baseline than nature. The great equalizer. Sixty years later profoundly rational men like *Scientific American* editor Gerard Piel were striking much the same theme, declaring the real value of wild places to be as reminders of the promise of a just society.

In the end, then, millions of people came to imagine the Rockies as being filled with simplicity and equality, precisely because those were the things most lacking in their daily lives. Such cravings allowed men like Ernest Thompson Seton, John Burroughs, and John Muir to take center stage. "Climb the mountains and get their good tidings," Muir advised eager readers in an 1898 article on Yellowstone. "Nature's peace will flow into you as sunshine flows into trees. The winds will blow their freshness into you, and the storms their energy, while cares will drop off like autumn leaves." Many not only were hugely sympathetic to Muir's poetic point of view but often seemed willing to go him one better, reawakening an old fondness for utterly ethereal visions of nature. Even that favorite motif of transcendent mystery—the little people, the invisibles—rose again in the early twentieth century to claim the public imagination. Visitors to Yellowstone in the 1920s, for example, gathered in great throngs on summer evenings to watch a piece of theater consisting of park employees dressed as sprites and nymphs, frolicking about in the waters of Apollonaris Spring.

Even clergy got into the act. In a sermon at the First Presbyterian Church of Portland, Oregon, the Reverend Dr.

E. P. Hill waxed poetic to his parishioners about a recent trip to Yellowstone. "Think of standing on the shore [of Yellowstone Lake] . . . and seeing bears walking composedly through the forests and graceful deer coming down fearlessly to the brink and stepping in without thought of danger, as if the day promised by the prophet had come, when man and beast of forest shall dwell together. . . . The mountains are covered with pink and purple and gold. The sky is an ocean of lavender, in which great white ships are sailing off to the city of God. Down there in the cities, where sin and sickness and sorrow stalk the streets, and men are engaged in their never-ending strife, we have seen the world as man has transformed it. Here, in this place of peace and purity and beauty, we see the world as God made it."

Rather than focusing on the dangerous aspects of nature as a means of building character, writers such as Muir and preachers like Hill characterized it as relief for the tired, nerve-shaken, and overcivilized. Thousands of people, Muir wrote in the *Atlantic Monthly,* "are beginning to find out that going to the mountains is going home: that wilderness is a necessity, and that mountain parks and reservations are useful not only as fountains of timber and irrigation rivers, but as fountains of life." Even those who sought scenery in its most artificial forms, he said, "mixed with spectacles, silliness, and Kodaks; its devotees arrayed more gorgeously than scarlet tanagers, frightening the wild game with red umbrellas—even this is encouraging, and may well be regarded as a hopeful sign of the times."

Women writers of the day were often more forceful still. "If you are normal and philosophical," wrote Mary Roberts Rinehart, "if you love your country, if you are willing to learn how little you count in the eternal scheme of things, go ride in the Rocky Mountains and save your soul." Thousands showed themselves willing to take her advice. And more often than not, they found their best chance waiting at the front gate of the nearest dude ranch.

CHAPTER

The Coming of
the Dudes

Valley Ranch Brochure

Dude ranches had something for everyone. Especially notable was the
opportunity they offered wealthy girls and young women to escape the
sharp social confines of the Victorian era.

Are you feeling sick? Liver out of sorts? Tired when you get out of bed? Coffee tasteless? Toast half cold? Scold the kids? Snap at your stenographer and threaten to fire the office boy? Don't consult a doctor; there is a surer cure. Let old Doc Nature prescribe for you. . . . Don't set the alarm clock. You will awake at daybreak without it and leap from bed wide awake, with more pep than you've had in months. For heaven's sake, don't shave! Merely neglecting to shave will help start the day right. At dusk you will be boyishly weary. At night you will sink softly into slumber, filled with the peace of the woods, trees, mountains, sunlight and flowing water. . . .

—from a 1930s brochure by Karst's Rustic Camp, Gallatin Gateway, Montana

IF EVER THERE WAS A NEAR-PERFECT STAGE for playing out these differing visions of wild nature—one challenging, the other restorative—it was in the cookhouses, cabins, and corrals of the Rocky Mountain dude ranch. What was to become one of the most significant recreational movements in the country began in the late 1800s with barely a whisper, by way of the inexhaustible, and at first entirely free, hospitality offered up well east of the mountains by a pair of brothers named Eaton, who were only too happy to keep the latchstring out for wealthy eastern friends at their ranch in the badlands of North Dakota. A particularly enthusiastic letter by Howard Eaton to one of those friends ended up being published in a New York newspaper, where it was seen by none other than Teddy Roosevelt. Having recently suffered the loss of both his mother and his wife (both women died on the same day), the future president was ripe for the solace of the West. He wasted no time packing his trunks and heading off to North Dakota, where he soon bought the Maltese Cross Ranch near the Eaton brothers, thus beginning years of hunting and exploring up and down the Rockies.

The dawn of the twentieth century saw the dude ranch movement expanding fast through Montana, Wyoming, and Colorado—and later into New Mexico—forming the bulwark of many local economies long after the financial glory days of ranching were but a distant memory. Like every other aspect of the Rocky Mountain tourist scene, it was fueled by a nation consumed by thoughts of nature. Fresh Air camps, launched quietly in 1873 to help disadvantaged city kids, were twenty years later serving well over half a million children. Nature writing of one sort or another dominated magazines from the *Atlantic Monthly* to *Collier's*, while bookstore shelves sagged under the weight of authors like Henry David Thoreau and John Muir, John Burroughs, Ernest Thompson Seton, Teddy Roosevelt, and William Long. By 1900 Burroughs's children's readers could be found in nearly every school in America; just outside those same classrooms school gardens were proliferating, as more and more educators declared the earth itself an essential teaching tool. Tens of thousands of boys awoke on Christmas

morning thrilled to find Seton's *Wild Animals I Have Known*
waiting under the tree. Even psychology was on top of the
wave, as celebrated therapist G. Stanley Hall—the man who
made popular the term "adolescence"—made clear in 1906.
"In our urban hothouse life that tends to ripen everything
before its time, we must teach nature. . . . Two staples, stories and nature . . . constitute fundamental education." *Century Magazine* offered in 1905 that the movement had taken
on the aspect of a cult "which has no counterpart" anywhere
in the world.

The Eatons notwithstanding, many of the early dude
ranches had been established by wealthy hunting enthusiasts
from eastern America, Europe, and England, heading west
by the dozen with guns in hand to partake in the rugged
sporting life. By the end of the century a surprising number
of powerful men—including the Earl of Dunraven, British
gentry Moreton Frewen, and the noted London capitalist
Sir John Pender—had all acquired hunting lodges in or near
the mountains. It took little time before they too were being
visited by gaggles of influential friends, many of whom went
on to purchase their own spreads, in the process building the
backbone of both traditional and dude ranching throughout
the Rockies. Some of what are properly called dude ranches
today were in their early years teaching facilities for instruct-
ing the sons of wealthy Englishmen how to become ranchers, a service for which the owners were paid in the
neighborhood of five hundred dollars per year.

These were men who understood well Teddy Roosevelt's later claim that had it not been for his experiences in the West, he would never have been president. It wasn't only that a person gained strength and vigor by seeking adventure in the "wide, waste spaces of the earth," as Roosevelt put it. More to the point, such activity was critical to building character. "Nowadays," Roosevelt wrote in 1900, "whatever other faults the son of rich parents may tend to develop, he is at least forced by the opinion of all his associates of his own age to bear himself well in manly exercises and to develop his body—and therefore, to a certain extent, his character—in the rough sports which call for pluck, endurance, and physical address." The Rockies, concluded Roosevelt and many others, called for all three. (Roosevelt was often irritated by those who suggested his time out west was frivolous play; to him such outings—especially his time spent on the ranch—was plain old-fashioned hard work.) While travelers of means were taking to ranches, thousands of other, less wealthy adventurers were roaming the Rockies, too. Young men especially wandered more or less aimlessly at various times of the year, going for the sake of going, engaging in what locals called "stampedes"—the term having roughly the same meaning as "road trip" does today. Lacking well-heeled friends, their accommodations consisted of either a blanket on the ground or a flea-bitten room on a run-down ranch. Writing of a stampede in 1864, Joseph Warren Arnold tells of sleeping on a bunk containing a handful of Montana feathers, the furniture made up of a pile of rubbish in the corner of the room with a small sack of flour on top. "Supper being announced, we sat down and ate a burnt biscuit or two and a slice of good old strong bacon and drank a cup of coffee which was a little water colored with burnt crusts of bread. All this we got for the sum of one dollar and a quarter in gold dust."

In time such activity—especially that of more prominent, high-profile men like Roosevelt—helped shift the public's attention away from stories about guides, scouts, and trappers, all of which had created an avalanche of pulp fiction following the Civil War, onto a new kind of hero called the cowboy. From the 1890s on Americans couldn't get enough, launching a raft of work for writers of the range, most of whom had far less interest in reporting facts than in fueling myth. Never mind, for example, that a working cowboy would almost never be found with a gun on his hip. For one thing, it was too easy to trip the trigger when holding the lead rope of a trailing horse. The mythical cowboy needed a six-shooter because of the power it gave him to overwhelm the evil that sometimes lurked in unkempt places. Never mind too the incredible degree to which cowboying was predicated on a mix of sweat and tedium. Or even that while wranglers may have been free to change employers, they were for the most part company men, paid paltry wages to keep profits flowing to corporations anchored thousands of miles away. It was a powerful mix of wish and fantasy, one destined to continue right into modern times. As the tag line of a recent cowboy-style magazine ad for Marlboro cigarettes declared, "He's his own man, in a world he owns."

The dude ranch, then, was a mirror of the Rockies themselves—a land of dreams. As one unnamed dude rancher put it, people were leading increasingly complex lives, which meant they needed places to indulge primitive and heroic tastes. It was a simple formula, he explained in a 1926 article in *Sunset* magazine. "We give the dude a horse, we show him thirty thousand acres of land, sagebrush and mountains and woods and trout streams, and we say to him: Now Mister these are yours as long as you want to stay. Be just as wild as you like. Lose yourself if you want to. You needn't come to meals unless you get hungry. Only don't get killed and have a heart for your horse." Some ranches took all this a step further, actually creating clubs that sound a lot like adult versions of the Boy Scouts. At Montana's Nine Quarter Circle Ranch guests who displayed a high proficiency in tests of horsemanship, woodcraft, and camping skills received a set of silver spurs—"the presentation of which," promises a camp brochure, "is attended by the secret and mysterious ritual of the Na-ba-ghuah ceremony."

Both the cowboy and the dude ranch spoke loud and clear to the imaginations of hundreds of thousands of city dwellers, many of whom seemed desperate for images of someone astride a horse, riding through open country, free and confident. People were frantic for heroes like "the Virginian," a character dreamed up by easterner Owen Wister, a summa cum laude graduate of Harvard who was himself a regular visitor to the dude ranches of Wyoming. Wister, who suffered from mysterious health problems, was like so many others of the day urged by his doctor to spend time in the more invigorating climate of the West. He first stayed in Wyoming with Major and Mrs. Frank Wolcott, delighting in taking daily baths in the cold waters of Deer Creek. He eventually gave up his law practice to write full-time, heading west again and again to camp and hunt and study Indians, often staying at the JY Dude Ranch in Jackson Hole. "The Virginian"—known by no other name—while working as the foreman of a Wyoming cattle ranch, is forced to defend both the law and his honor against a rustler named Trampas, and the story ends with one of fiction's very first showdown gun battles. To readers of the day he was the picture of rugged individuality—defender of law, friends, and family—a man of few words and plenty of action.

But dude ranches also pulled in thousands of people who saw the Rockies not as a place for heroics, but as a source of inspiration and respite. This was the group celebrated Wyoming dude rancher Struthers Burt had in mind in 1927, when he described his job as "giving people homemade bedsteads but forty pound mattresses." They were people seeking breaks from the city not because it had a softening influence, but because it had a stifling one. Their lives felt out of balance, too much in service of productivity. They were in full agreement with the much admired preacher Henry Ward Beecher, who speculated that Americans were "dropping dead from the violence done to the brain by excessive industry."

The biggest challenge dude ranching faced, especially during the period from roughly 1885 to 1915, was to advertise itself with just the right mix of wild and civilized images. The majority of books and magazine articles about the region during the 1800s had been thick with stories of danger—hunters fending off grizzlies, Indian attacks, drunken fights in mining towns. And while all that proved highly entertaining, it did little to support the notion of coming west for a family vacation. Thus in the early twentieth century travel writers began focusing not so much on the danger of the place as on such unheard-of topics as the high degree of refinement and decorum in the locals. Writing about the Rocky Mountain dude rancher for *Collier's* in 1913, Jesse Williams claims that "the most significant thing of all is the inherent gentility of strong men who have got beyond the immediate influence of the funny little ideals of our permeating pecuniary culture. It is so different from artificial gentility." Men of propriety—but at the same time men who would forever stand against a backdrop of unbridled land. "Here tired ponies have squirmed at loosened girths to wheel into the sage for supper," recounts one ranch brochure from the 1930s. "And here the cook has bellowed out the back door and banged the irons. Forty years of it. And the stars still pop like hot bullets, and coyotes still rim the silences with wailing."

It was an era when many Americans perused their dude

ranch brochures by winter, headed for the mountains in summer, and in their spare time used their passion for the great outdoors to turn naturalists into full-blown pop idols. Nature writer John Burroughs, traveling with President Roosevelt to Yellowstone in 1903, found at every train station hundreds of schoolchildren smiling, shouting, holding welcome banners meant just for him. So too did these same children and their parents take to heart with unflinching devotion naturalist Ernest Thompson Seton, carrying him from a struggling life on the Canadian prairie to the ranks of American celebrity. Seton in particular seemed to light fires in thousands of people who then went off to slake their desire on the doorsteps of the dude ranch. His success was in part due to a commitment to blend painstaking observation—the scientific, if you will—with unabashed passion. He was a naturalist, purred the *New York Times Book Review* in 1940, "as opposed to the colder-blooded scientist."

All this isn't to say that Seton's animal stories—for a time, part of the most successful genre in American publishing—didn't raise an occasional eyebrow. At one point fellow naturalist John Burroughs blew up at him, writing an article in the *Atlantic Monthly* calling Seton "a fraud, a faker, a sham naturalist." It was the opening salvo in what turned out to be a five-year conflict known as the war of the nature fakers. At the height of the skirmish Burroughs and then president Teddy Roosevelt were writing dozens of letters back and forth bitterly denouncing the fakers—most especially William Long, whose books were in schools and libraries across the country, and who routinely ascribed humanlike characteristics to animals. Despite Roosevelt's intention to remain above the fray, to protect the office of the presidency by confining his remarks to private letters and conversations, he seemed unable to play it close to the vest. The debate soon spilled into the national press, with each naturalist firing salvos at those who would dare besmirch his name. The *New York Times* called it the literary war of the century.

Burroughs had been right in this sense: there were definitely writers who were more than happy to ascribe all sorts of ludicrous behaviors to wildlife, scribbling out great rafts of nonsense simply to feed the public's insatiable hunger for natural history. Yet in the end Burroughs came to regret including Seton in his tirade, offering a red-faced apology when the two men crossed paths at a literary dinner party at the home of Andrew Carnegie. Burroughs was further chagrined three weeks later, standing in Seton's home at Cos Cob, Connecticut, gazing at a five-thousand-volume science library, three thousand bird and mammal skins Seton had personally collected and mounted, more than a thousand drawings, and thirty volumes of observation journals. In time Seton would go on to win the Gold Medal of the American Academy of Sciences for his *Lives of Game Animals,* and ironically, the John Burroughs Memorial Association award for outstanding work in zoology. (While Seton was forever personalizing animals, he was no Walt Disney. An accomplished artist, he submitted for the Chicago

World's Fair in 1893 a startling painting set in western Canada called *Triumph of the Wolves,* depicting a pack of wolves devouring the last of a hapless woodsman. Far from being a diatribe against wolves—indeed, Seton helped pave the way for the public to embrace the role of predators—it was a nonchalant if improbable narrative about life and death in the natural world. The arts committee, concerned that people would get the wrong idea about Canadian rural life, asked him not only to retouch the piece but to rename it. Thus the painting was finally released not as *Triumph of the Wolves* but as *Waiting in Vain: A Scene in the Pyrenees,* hung so high on the wall of the exhibition hall that visitors could barely see it.)

Though most people considered Seton a member of that second camp of nature lovers, who saw wild places as a healing force, he was a bit like Roosevelt in that he considered nature the best place of all for building character, especially in children. With the success of *Wild Animals I Have Known,* which eventually sold a phenomenal 500,000 copies, Seton began focusing on a longstanding dream to build an outdoor organization for young boys—a means, he said, of channeling their natural love of glory, gang instinct, and need for ritual into the behaviors of well-adjusted young men. In a 1902 article in *Ladies' Home Journal* he announced the formation of a group called the Woodcraft Indians; anyone interested could obtain a 400-page book he'd written, *The Birch Bark Roll,* which included organizational details as well as explanations of a merit badge system for natural science, outdoor cooking, and other achievements. Chapters sprung up overnight—not just in America but in Canada, England, South Africa, Poland, and Czechoslovakia.

When the commander in chief of the British army got wind of the organization, he directed General Robert Stephenson Smyth Baden-Powell to help Seton anchor the movement in the British Isles; six years later Baden-Powell announced the founding of the Boy Scouts, an obvious knockoff of the Woodcraft Indians. The organizational structure of bands, tribes, and medicine men Seton dreamt up became under Baden-Powell patrols, troops, and scout-masters. Seton's advice to "do at least one act of unselfish service each day" became under the Boy Scout banner, "A scout must do a good turn every day." "Be a friend to all harmless wild life" was turned into the Boy Scout code of "A scout is a friend to animals." While the founding of the Boy Scouts has long been attributed to Baden-Powell, many prominent Englishmen of the day strongly urged Seton to step up to the plate and take honors they felt rightfully belonged to him. But Seton was never one to encourage controversy; indeed, he'd never even responded in print to Burroughs's charge that he was a nature faker. Instead, in 1910 he became chair of the committee to organize the Boy Scouts of America, then went on to become chief scout and write the first scout manual.

In the end, though, Seton grew irritated by what he considered an overemphasis by the Boy Scouts on mili-tarism—a current that picked up considerable force with the advent of World War I. For their part, the Boy Scouts seemed increasingly nervous about Seton's heavy emphasis on Native American life, not to mention his reputation as a pacifist. Seton would resign—some say he was kicked out, the official reason being that he was a Canadian citizen— only to rekindle in 1915 the original Woodcraft group. This time it was called the Woodcraft League of America—coeducational, and open to all ages. Seton founded the Brownies six years later, which was later adopted by close friends and founders of the Camp Fire Girls, Mr. and Mrs. Luther Glick.

In short, Seton, Burroughs, Roosevelt, William Long, and dozens of other writers had a great deal to do with why parents were incredibly eager to carry their children west, to the dude ranches of the Rockies. Magazine writers routinely espoused the idea of dude ranch vacations for teenagers, some making the point that leading an active life in the boondocks would keep them safe from dangerous parties, illicit drinking, and all the other temptations of youth. Even men in their twenties were strongly encouraged to visit the ranches of the Rockies—not so much to avoid temptation as to dry out. In truth, things didn't always work out that way. Writing in 1930, author Hermann Hagedorn describes how "the dudes regularly came back from town with all [the alcohol] they could carry without and within; and the cowboys round about swore solemnly that you couldn't put your hand in the crotch of any tree within a hundred yards of the . . . ranch house without coming upon a bottle concealed by a dude being cured of the drink."

DUDE RANCHES SEEM MOST INTRIGUING when viewed in
the context of their other role, which was as a refuge for
black sheep. Much as had happened during the days of the
mountain man, in this era too there came streaming into the
mountains sons of wealthy easterners and Europeans, sent
west not just to fuel their dreams of playing cowboy but just
as often to keep them away from the delicate social maneu-
verings of the family. Remittance men, they came to be
called, so named for the regular checks, or remittances, sent
by parents back home to keep them firmly planted in some
saddle far away. "He may have an unquenchable thirst, his
mental IQ may at times lean a little toward the minus side,"
says Wyoming writer Mary Shawver of the remittance man.
"It may be any number of things that Sister may think impedes
her progress toward the inner circle of the Astorbilts."

Men like Clement Stuart Bengough. Son of an
extraordinarily affluent English family, Bengough was too
shy to navigate even the most basic social situations, choosing to spend all his time either outdoors or closeted in his
room at the palatial family estate in Gloucestershire. At age
twenty-five Bengough's father handed him a sizable check
and told him to pack his bags and go find his place in the
world. As fate would have it, Clement ended up in
Wyoming, signing on at a dude ranch which, like many in
the 1880s, specialized in training wealthy neophytes in the
art and science of running cattle. He proved well suited to
the life, eventually buying land and livestock for an operation of his own. His modest spread in western Wyoming,

south of Jackson, included a small cabin with an outstanding library, from which he routinely wrote letters in Latin to his beloved sisters living abroad in England and South Africa. Never once did Bengough return to England, passing up even the chance to lay claim to a $300,000 estate left to him by an uncle.

Often the sons of well-heeled easterners would buy places in the Rockies but occupy them only seasonally, going to great lengths to keep the two worlds separated. Wealthy Bostonian James Boyd spent much of the year running cattle in Colorado, living in a rough-cut timber cabin on the Arkansas River with a sod roof and clay floor. He arrived in the region during a particularly raucous era, when thugs of all stripes were roaming the countryside ostensibly for the purpose of rounding up wild horses, yet were only too happy to take private stock if no wild ones were about. Boyd's letters back east are cautious, reserved, giving confused relatives little insight into what kept drawing him to the mountains—agreeing that, yes, after a winter in Boston the West was hard to get used to. "I can assure you that when one travels here . . . in a comfortable Pullman car and then steps off on to the station platform in a small Colorado cattle town and is welcomed by a rough crowd of men in high boots, flannel shirts, slouch hats and of general uncouth appearance, he finds the change and contrast very great." To his friends in the Rockies, meanwhile, Boyd barely mentions his life back east at all. Then again, by all appearances he at least avoided Charlie Russell's game of writing letters to western friends with intentionally misspelled words, thereby downplaying his wealthy eastern origins.

Running the nearby saloon, meanwhile, was one of Boyd's neighbors—a thirty-five-year-old New Yorker named Dickenson, yet another man who said next to nothing about his life back east to cowboy friends and customers. Boyd took Dickenson to be a man of considerable education and refinement, though he also noted that his saloon job required working with a couple of revolvers under the counter in case trouble broke out. "Every summer," writes Boyd, "he would go East and enjoy a yachting trip on quite a large and beautiful yacht of which he was part owner. Whether his associates in the East knew how he made his money and occupied his time during the balance of the years or not, I never knew." Similarly driven was Malcom Mackay of Englewood, New Jersey, son of the head of the New York Stock Exchange, who as a boy lived with his family in a mansion of some three dozen rooms. As a young man Malcom turned his back on all that, heading west to the Beartooth Mountains of Montana. "He'd go back home fairly often," explains his granddaughter, Julia Childs. "But it was as though he was living a double life."

There came as well to the dude ranch hundreds of wealthy young women—for a time called dudines—many of them black sheep in their own right, seeking relief from the harsh social mores still lingering from the Victorian era. In the latter years of the nineteenth century and well into the twentieth, people of means tended to escape the smoke and simmer of New York summers by heading upstate to any of several posh resorts located in the Catskills and on the Atlantic shore. Such places expected their female guests not only to have extensive wardrobe changes, including formal wear for dinner, but to engage only in passive activities— playing croquet or cards, reading or conversing quietly on the porch. On matters of fashion alone the dude ranch offered these women an astonishing breath of fresh air, requiring not corsets and crinoline and petticoats, but jeans and boots and Stetson hats. As the decades passed, more and more women jumped ship, until finally even the fashion magazines were forced to give their stamp of approval. A 1934 article in *Vogue* titled "Dressing the Dude" assured women that the Rockies was a place where wardrobe concerns were easily met with wool socks, blue jeans, flannel shirts, and practical underwear. One way to earn the praise of westerners, the article advises, is to dress neither like a Madison Square trick-roper nor like a Long Island horsewoman. The *New York Times* gave a nod to the movement no questions asked, conceding that "lately the dude ranch has taken its place in the social calendar as a thing that one must do, and the social register lists dilatory domiciles in Montana and Wyoming along with those in Southampton and Antibes."

But comfortable clothing was just the beginning. In the Rockies women dined at large tables with the men, free to participate in every conversation. At the drop of a Stetson they could roll up their sleeves to go round up cattle, learn a new rodeo move, spend an afternoon with a fast horse or a fly rod instead of perched on the veranda making small talk and fluttering their hand fans. (Those hand fans, by the way, provide a curious glimpse into the bizarre cloak of Victorian mores that had proliferated in high society beginning at roughly mid-century. A woman fanning slow was said to be declaring that she was engaged, while a fast motion was to convey independence; resting the fan on the right cheek meant yes, the left cheek, no, and the fan held by the right hand in front of the face meant the observer was to follow. All of this was neither understood nor endorsed by cowboy culture. Little wonder one Montana dude rancher at the turn of the century claimed his wealthy guests needed a full month to peel away the strictures of their lives back home.) Such girls had spent years at fashionable private schools, explained dude ranch owner Helen Brooke Hereford, training for eastern society life. "They enjoyed themselves to the limit here on the ranch. Instead of the pretty clothes they were used to they wore blue jeans . . . leading a simple life without so-called social activities. They left declaring enthusiastically [that they'd had] the best time of their lives."

It may seem odd to think of "dudines" finding freedom in a part of the country that even now can seem overwhelmed by testosterone. But the Rockies was known early on as being friendly to the idea of enfranchising women. Admittedly, such moves were to no small degree meant to attract additional settlers, thereby advancing the quest for statehood. But it's also true that there was simply less opposition to such ideas in the Rocky Mountain West. Wyoming led the nation in woman's suffrage, adopting right-to-vote laws in 1869, while still a territory. When Congress later told the territorial legislature that its application for statehood would never pass so long as suffrage was allowed, Wyoming snubbed them. "We will remain out of the Union a hundred years," declared one legislator, "rather than come in without the women." In 1869 Susan B. Anthony put out a call for eastern women to migrate en masse to Wyoming; though relatively few responded, she and Elizabeth Cady Stanton headed out for a long look in 1871, traveling on the newly completed Transcontinental Railroad. Utah, meanwhile, enacted suffrage only a year behind Wyoming, followed by Colorado and finally Idaho, in 1896—two decades before the passage of the Nineteenth Amendment. (Women weren't the only ones able to breathe a little easier in the mountains. In the 1930s one-third to one-half of the guest resorts in the eastern United States were restricted, banning both Jews and blacks—policies almost unheard of in the Rockies.)

Encouraging women's rush to the mountains were books like *A Woman Tenderfoot*, by Ernest Thompson Seton's influential feminist wife, Grace. Part narrative, part instruction manual for women of means, the work is the story of a long ramble through the Rockies on an extended hunting and photography trip with her husband at the end of the nineteenth century. Being a woman of some privilege herself, Grace was hardly unfamiliar with the more unsavory aspects of high-society resort vacations. As for posh summer hotels, she found particularly irritating the degree of self-consciousness women seemed to bring along—worries that left them on edge about social position, manners, acceptable dress. "Do you not get enough of that life in the winter to last all year?" she asks in the early pages of *A Woman Tenderfoot*. "A possible mosquito or gnat in the mountains is no more irritating than the objectionable personality that is sure to be forced upon you every hour at the summer hotel. The usual walk, the usual drive, the usual hop, the usual novel, the usual scandal. . . ."

The fact that Grace Seton Thompson had taken her share of high teas in refined places makes her struggles in the mountains all the more fascinating. Lost in the high country with Ernest late one evening, she comes to understand the danger of panic. "Always regulate your fears according to the situation," she tells her readers, "and then you will not go into the valley of the shadow of death, when you are only lost in the mountains." She also comes to appreciate how conditions change lightning fast in the wilderness—that one can either remain open to the adventure of such change or be overcome by fear. One thing is certain about a woman who chooses to rough it, she offers: "There is no compromise. She either sits in the lap of happiness or of misery. The two are side by side, and toss about her about a dozen times a day—but happiness never lets her go for long."

While much of her writing is clearly anchored to the

postures of the era, it features no small amount of grit and endurance, the very things taught in the Teddy Roosevelt school of character development. To most wealthy women of the day such notions were so unfamiliar as to be downright shocking. Riding for hours through a blinding snowstorm in the Wind River Range, her first impulse is to break down, but this she fights against with enormous determination. "Don't be a cry-baby," she mutters to herself over and over. "There is lots of good stuff in you yet. This only seems terrible because you are not used to it, so brace up." In this way she spends an entire afternoon—clenching her teeth, growing more chilled with each passing hour, her horse plodding through ever deeper snow. But she makes it, and manages a lot of other things as well—from surviving a hell-for-leather run across the prairie with a spooked horse, to fending off a rattlesnake with an iron skillet. Grace wasn't kidding in the early pages of *A Woman Tenderfoot* when she invites her readers to "come with me and learn how to be vulgarly robust."

As the book closes, it's clear Grace regrets nothing about her time in the Rockies. She talks of having hunted much and killed a little, of learning from people she met what it means to be a miner, a cowboy, of having caught her breath on waking and finding the tracks of a mountain lion barely three feet from where she'd laid her head. "But best of all," she says in lines that are revolutionary, "I have felt the charm of the glorious freedom, the quick rushing blood, the bounding motion of the wild life, the joy of the living and of the doing, of the mountain and the plain; I have learned to know and feel some, at least, of the secrets of the Wild Ones. In short, though I am still a woman and may be tender, I am a Woman Tenderfoot no longer."

Admittedly, such displays of strength in women weren't encouraged by everyone. In a letter dated December 1915 to the acting superintendent of Yellowstone, F. J. Haynes of the Yellowstone Western Stage Company recalls a unique strategy employed by a stagecoach driver to foil a robbery in the park earlier in the year. The driver, Haynes explains, carrying ten women from New York, "suggested to the ladies that perhaps the road agent would not hold them up if they would cry. Which worked successfully, as the highwayman said 'Drive on with that bunch of babies,' and they were not molested."

Among those young women who took Grace Seton's advice and made for the mountains, a surprising number would come to stay in the Rockies, falling in love and marrying the sons of ranch owners or their foremen. From a business standpoint such couplings proved enormously valuable, since these women provided not just operating capital for the dude ranch but, just as important, a large pool of eastern family and friends from which to draw their guests. This in turn freed their western husbands to focus on running livestock, building cabins, managing pastures, hiring and training wranglers. Many traditional livestock ranches are today in the hands of the original family only because wealthy eastern girls married into the operations, saving them with inheritances during droughts, killing winters, and the ravages of the Depression.

Whether it happened by marriage or other kinds of partnerships, this blending of eastern capital and connections with western know-how was a powerful mix. Princeton graduate Larry Larom made a great success of the Valley Ranch in Cody, Wyoming, thanks in no small part to the help of western wranglers and guides. On the other hand, when he decided to expand his operations to include a college prep school for boys, filling the slots meant leaning hard on connections at his alma mater, as well as on those of his partners, who'd graduated from Colgate and Yale. For the rather pricey sum of $1,550 a year students sat in the shadows of the Absaroka Range and worked through a full academic roster, which included everything from Latin to physics. Classes were taught by professors from Harvard, Penn State, and Princeton. There was also an eclectic mix of extracurricular activities—from soccer to fishing, polo to trapping. Each boy was required to furnish his own quality .22 caliber rifle.

This sort of diversification was yet another way dude ranches weathered tough economic times. Surely the most inspired example occurred west of the Rockies, at the Lazy M Ranch near Reno, Nevada, where Cornelius Vanderbilt was in the 1920s attracting an enthusiastic clientele of movie stars from Clark Gable to Amelia Earhart, Will Rogers, Charlie Chaplin, Gary Cooper, and Douglas Fairbanks Jr. When business began to slow in the early 1930s, Vanderbilt started offering what Lawrence Borne calls the "package ranch divorce." The gimmick was created to take advantage of the fact that it took only six weeks to gain Nevada residency, at which point a person could dissolve a failing marriage with little more than the stroke of a pen. For $795 Vanderbilt provided room and board for those six weeks at the Lazy M Ranch, throwing in a horse to ride, a good supply of cigarettes, two trips each week to Reno, and a free bottle of liquor.

GIVEN THAT MOST EARLY DUDE RANCHERS were started, or at least partnered, by well-educated sportsmen, it comes as no surprise that many would prove deeply committed to conservation, often trumping those who would plunder the land for quick profits. Dude ranchers carried weight—in part because they were considered locals (to this day that counts for a lot in the rural West) but also because they provided an economic base in regions either struggling financially or at best subject to the brutal boom-and-bust cycles of extractive industry. When dude ranchers spoke, people listened. One of their first victories came early in the twentieth century, as thousands of elk were being poached for their so-called ivory teeth, or tusks. At that time the civic group the Fraternal Order of Elk was enormously popular, their members eager to see elk teeth turned into everything from cuff links to watch charms. It was in large part dude ranchers in the Jackson Hole region who finally convinced Elk lodges across the country to stop using the teeth, which in turn helped ease the slaughter. Such efforts helped endear dude ranchers to state game commissioners, even if the two groups often disagreed about what constituted proper land management. "Most of our meetings are held with irate farmers," explained Wyoming game commissioner John Scott in 1932, "[or with] hunters who come . . . firmly set against the game commission and game laws. So it is a mighty fine feeling to know that you come to a meeting where the people are kindred spirits."

Dude ranchers in general were acutely aware of the fragile nature of the wild. They were among the first to express opposition to the overcommercialization of the national parks—a position that quickly found its way into the popular press. By 1919 the cry to throttle back development was being sounded in a variety of mainstream publications, including the *Saturday Evening Post*. "Selling scenery is a dangerous business," writes editor George Horace Lorimer. "To popularize our national parks without destroying the very thing that we are trying to save, is a job that calls for unusual qualities."

The founding constitution of the Dude Ranchers' Association called for members to "work with the federal government for the conservation and preservation of parks and forests, and the conservation and protection of wildlife." In the 1930s the organization not only continued to speak out against the commercialization of the parks but, more remarkable still, came out dead set against the diversion of water for agriculture. A decade later ranchers like Larry

Larom were raising the roof in Washington, D.C., testifying before Congress against a scheme often floated by property rights militants in the Rockies, calling for federal lands to be turned over to the states, then ultimately to individuals. Such a move would all but guarantee, argued the dude ranchers (without a hint of irony), that the best of Wyoming would end up in the hands of the rich.

The prevailing attitude of the era was summed up well by feisty Helen Brooke Hereford, from her guest ranch at the foot of Montana's Beartooth Mountains. "I'm not a sloppy sentimental sort of person," she writes, "but what mountains and simple mountain life does to one is just hard to put into words, and is foolish to try. It is going to be a crime if the mountains are not kept as natural as they are. They cannot be improved." In a region where locals often view the hunger and influence of people from the urban East as a form of colonialism, the dude ranch was for a time as close to the best of both worlds as the West would ever get. More than any other vacation experience before or since, there was in the dude ranch an extraordinary level of intimacy between guests and owners. Dude ranch owners routinely traveled in the winter months to New York, Boston, Philadelphia, and Chicago, where former guests hosted gatherings to introduce them to prospective clients. Christmas cards and chatty newsletters from the ranchers were common fare, helping to sustain relationships that families would come to cherish for generations. Best estimates are that over half of all dude ranch visitors were returning guests from previous years, while many of the rest were friends and relatives.

By the mid-1920s there were nearly seventy-five dude ranches in Colorado, Montana, and Wyoming; within a decade they were entertaining more than fifteen thousand people annually, adding millions of dollars annually to local economies. So successful was the movement that a great many entrepreneurs back east decided to create dude ranches of their own. A *New York Times* article describes one of these businessmen, apparently desperate for a little western flavor, buying a single buffalo from the Central Park Zoo and tying it to the horse corral for guests to ogle.

As far as locals were concerned, the timing of all this couldn't have been better. Cattle prices had been plummeting since roughly 1919; at the same time the cost of raising beef was swelling in the face of persistent drought, forcing higher prices for hay. Up and down the mountains ranches were being abandoned. Given such hardships, some traditional ranchers took a step they'd never wanted to, opening their doors to dudes—offering not so much the full menu of recreational opportunities available elsewhere in the Rockies as the simple chance for an out-of-stater to put on a cowboy hat, climb on a horse, and ride along as part of regular operations. Again, the big attraction of such a vacation, even among the wealthy, was that it offered the chance to eat trail dust and burn a few saddle sores. Test the mettle. The idea of installing comforts like indoor bathrooms and telephones—at these ranches, or for that matter any other dude ranch in the Rockies—was soundly rejected by guests and owners alike, all of whom thought such convenience would erode the value of the experience. Some of the highest praise ever given the Eaton brothers came by way of Wyoming dude rancher Struthers Burt, who said they never forgot that what guests valued most was the somewhat peculiar life of the ranch itself. Well after they'd become prosperous, Burt says, with dude operations earning far more money than cattle, "they never made the mistake of turning the place into anything other than what it was."

In the years following World War II fast cars, paved roads, and a public pent up and ready to drive brought millions of new visitors to the mountains. Between 1940 and 1948 visitation to Rocky Mountain National Park increased 1,000 percent; likewise, from 1950 to 1964 national forest use grew more than 800 percent, from 1.5 million annually to more than 14.5 million. According to a publication released by Utah State University, between 1940 and 1960 the service industry in the mountain states grew at a rate five times as fast as the national average. The number of guest ranches in Colorado alone rose by close to 40 percent.

Yet for the most part the golden era of the dude ranch was over, as more and more owners found themselves scrambling to keep up with dramatic shifts in public expectations. The same modern conveniences that had been routinely shunned by guests thirty years earlier, considered crass tokens of modernity, were suddenly in big demand. Ranches that had led guests up mountain trails for a month or even six weeks at a time in 1920 were by 1950 offering breakfast and dinner rides lasting no more than a couple of hours. In Jackson during 1956 came the Dude-for-a-Day Ranch, where for ten dollars travelers could grab a riverside horseback ride and two meals and be on their way. Four years later the V-J Ranch of Jackson Hole, Wyoming, was advertising itself as "one of the few real working ranches left in the West." Instead of being eager to immerse themselves in the landscape, as had been the rule of the past, now dudes were content merely to look at it. "After all," writes Lawrence Borne, "they could see the mountains or forests or deserts; why did they have to go out into them?" If the dude ranches of the Rockies traced much of the story of America's hunger for the wild, following the Second World War they would chronicle society's growing impatience with what living and traveling in the wilderness really requires. In an era suddenly obsessed with speed and convenience, many of the things that had been most valued about such vacations were overwhelmed, until finally only the mountains themselves remained to remind the traveler that he'd traveled anywhere at all.

Ironically, as ranches scrambled to meet these changing expectations, there was at the same time a massive generation of baby boomers coming into the world, many of whom would go on to claim much the same hunger for a deep relationship to the land that had been part and parcel of the old dude ranch way. Yet as young adults, baby boomers tended to think of dude ranches as places offering exclusive vacations for establishment fat cats. They would come to the Rockies instead by thumb, by Chevy Impala and Volkswagen microbus, camping in Forest Service campgrounds, largely unaware that they were moving to rhythms that had been coursing through the culture for more than a century.

CHAPTER 9

Season of the Freaks

***Hippies on the Company Store Bench* (1970s)**
Like several other Rocky Mountain towns, between 1968 and 1973
Crested Butte went from a sleepy mining community to a haven for middle-
class youth—in particular, those looking for an alternative to mainstream
society.

THE THIRTY-SOMETHING WOMAN ON THE end stool at the bar is new in town, barely two weeks out from her former life in Chicago. She sips cabernet and tells the rest of us how Crested Butte was the first mountain town she ever laid eyes on, way back when she was just eleven. But that was vacation, she explains, and this is serious. This is starting over. Starting over from what isn't exactly clear. During lulls in the conversation she trades jokes, flirts with a waiter in his late twenties moving with great energy across the scuffed wooden floor, serving burgers and salads, a guy named Jerry who himself came out from Minneapolis only a year ago to learn to snowboard, and never left. "He's got a Ph.D. in medieval history," the woman whispers, and her tone has a lot of "Imagine that!" in it. When she gets up to go to the bathroom, an athletic-looking guy roughly the same age pipes up from a nearby table, says you can tell the woman's new because she's holding on to one of the great delusions about mountain towns—namely, that people with Ph.D.'s take jobs waiting tables by choice. "In the beginning we look like renaissance men," he says quietly, downing a last swallow of bourbon. "But in the end we just look desperate."

When the woman returns the guy at the table catches her eye, a grin unfolding under his mustache. "Want to know the best way to make a small fortune in Crested Butte?" It's a joke, black humor, one I've heard told up and down the Rockies for years, including in my own mountain town five hundred miles to the north.

"No," she says suspiciously. "Tell me."

"Start with a big one."

Outside on Elk Avenue is a steady parade of well-coiffed men and women with tanned legs sticking out of cargo shorts, felt jackets draped across their shoulders. Small coveys of twenty-something men pass by, too, hands in their pockets and looking skyward, as if they might pull down an early snow. Locals ride by on clunker bikes. Black Labs and golden retrievers crisscross the street; a chocolate Lab sporting a red bandanna around his neck makes a beeline for the front door of the bar, trots in and vacuums the floor of peanuts, hurries back out to points unknown. Mayor Linda Ward is across the street and moving fast, talking to her neighbors on the fly, probably off to take care of some urgent matter at her toy store down the street. And there's Glo Cunningham, on her way to work the pledge drive at KBUT, never taking more than a couple dozen steps before having to stop for yet another conversation.

To this day there are still places you can find pieces of the Rocky Mountains of a century ago: lingering with the cigarette smoke at the Buckhorn bar in Laramie, where middle-aged cowboys tip bottles of beer, look to the west, and hope for rain. It's in the eager shouts of dudes on horseback, two days out from Turpin Meadows, drifting toward Hawks Rest and the Absaroka Divide. But mostly you'll find them in small towns. Communities within arm's reach of the high country, from northwest Montana all the way to central New Mexico. Ideally it should be a town with some variety—someplace where those pursuing fantasies haven't yet been swept away in the wake of those merely buying them. Some elderly mining widows, shopkeepers and mechanics and punk skiers, a few rich corporate dropout types, a plein air painter or two. And along with all that, hopefully a handful or two who still carry torches from the last big social movement to hit the Rockies—one of the most entertaining, if least celebrated, displays of American wildlands fever of the past seventy-five years, the back-to-nature movement of the late 1960s and early 1970s.

The young men and women who drove or flew or hitchhiked en masse into the Rockies thirty-some years ago stumbled into childhood at a time when Americans were spending over $100 million a year on cowboy hats, pistols, chaps, and other western paraphernalia for their kids—every vinyl gun belt, every cheap metal six-shooter and pair of cotton rodeo pajamas reinforcing the idea that life, at least life in the West, was no more complicated than a lonely trail, a nose for freedom, and a well-trained horse. Following years of western B movies, 1955 saw the premiere of *Gunsmoke, Cheyenne,* and *The Life and Legend of Wyatt Earp*—all destined to become top-ranking shows, with *Gunsmoke* claiming the number one slot in the country for three straight years. The 1958–59 television season brought a staggering twenty-five weekly westerns, and that number kept growing for several seasons. Even Walt Disney was doing his part, producing in 1948 the first of his enormously popular *True Life Adventure* shows. The second program in the series, filmed in the Rockies and called *Beaver Valley,* won the Academy Award for short subjects in 1950.

And then, of course, the teen years. An emerging back-to-nature movement, offering everything from color spreads in *Life* magazine on "The Coming of the Commune" to songs about running to the hills by everyone from Joe Walsh to Canned Heat, Joni Mitchell to John Prine. And run they did, being among the last in a long string of generations to sooth the angst of youth not with Ritalin, but with road trips. As often as not they were journeys to the mountain West. Places where you could lean on the throttle and gulp down space, hatch notions of freedom every bit as keen as any that had sprouted for real in the high valleys or along the sage-covered foothills of the Rockies.

The ease with which this generation pulled land-inspired fantasies out of their hats was in part due to the fact that even then the Rocky Mountains carried a natty sense of unsettledness, unpredictability—a kind of creative bedlam all but unknown back in the land of clipped lawns and swimming pools and Putt-Putt golf. Here were snowstorms in July, and in late summer, wind squalls powerful enough to knock down hundreds of acres of trees in a single breath. In late spring came the thunder of landslides ripping loose from the upper shoulders of the high country; normally modest creeks suddenly turned treacherous with melting snow. Almost as amazing as nature itself was how people who lived and worked in the mountains reacted to it, the drama of the land forging personalities that seemed somehow more expectant, outrageous. It wasn't just that the Rockies attracted ruffians and various others slightly off the bubble—though without question they did—but that they continued to allow peculiarities of thought that in other rural parts of the country would have been scowled at, censured, denounced.

If there's such a thing as a perfect snapshot of the back-to-nature movement of the 1960s and early 1970s, it's in Crested Butte, at Town Hall, framed in black plastic on the wall of council chambers. Here hangs the front page of the *Crested Butte Chronicle* from April 8, 1972, containing photos of the newly elected mayor and town council. The Honorable William (Van) Crank has just defeated incumbent mayor Lyle McNeil—a man who'd served as both councilman and mayor for some twenty-six years—by a vote of 220 to 163. Crank himself, the first mayor in the town's history to even sport a beard, looks like Levon Helm at the end of a Dylan tour. Newly elected councilman Roger Kahn is also in full beard, while Ron Baar stands with a skewed baseball hat, tilted coffee cup in his hand, eyes at half-mast. Then there's the boyish face of Tommy Glass, the matted hair and confident smile of Danny Gallagher, the pretty, smiling Kathleen Ross, her straight blond hair falling across a turtleneck sweater. And finally, the long-haired, mustached Jim Wallace, who in another eight months would be off to set dynamite charges for a slightly possessed German man on the prairies of South Dakota, determined to turn a mountain into a statue of Crazy Horse.

It was a victory made possible in large part by Crank's friends, who'd canvassed the bars cajoling hippies and ski bums to get out and vote. When the dust settled only one of the previous council members was left standing—himself a young newcomer who'd rolled into town just two years earlier. In that single election the political lineup of Crested Butte changed from a group of men whose lives spun around the price of coal and metal and beef to a group of mostly bright, laid-back former urbanites who truly believed that whatever was left of the American dream would be found, or at least reawakened, in a backwater mining town in the Colorado Rockies.

As writer Annie Gottlieb points out, nature served the 1960s generation on several levels. To begin with, the natural world provided refuge for religious feelings young people felt no longer needed to be tethered to a church pew. And while those spiritual sentiments might today seem peculiar, they were in truth nothing more or less than the latest spin on those same mythical motifs that had appeared over the centuries. There was, for example, at least among the more serious in the counterculture, a keen hope for community— a longing fanned to no small degree by the harsh, remote conditions of these mountains. In the late 1960s there was in Crested Butte no grocery store, no bank or television or daily paper. "We didn't even have phones," recalls Mayor Linda Ward. "We didn't have baby-sitters. And we didn't have money." Many who headed for the Rockies in the 1960s and early 1970s came looking for a life without the corrupting influences of the "system," but with a good supply of like-minded friends within arm's reach. "Nobody asked me what I was looking for when I showed up there in 1966," says George Sibley, former editor of the *Crested Butte Chronicle*. "If I'd thought about it long enough I would've said I'm looking for something different than what I'd known all my life. I was looking for community, and that's what I found. On the street. In the Grubstake Restaurant, where they had a $1.29 dinner special and every young person in town went there—old guys, too, sitting at the bar wondering who among us was going to last the winter. Community was all we had." They were looking for rumblings of transcendent mystery, too, often played out through the drug scene: long-haired painters playing flutes in the meadows near O-Be-Joyful Creek like some modern-day Thomas Cole; friends sitting cross-legged in sun-drenched meadows, high on acid. And of course there was beauty. Beauty everywhere you looked.

Theirs was a movement neither prompted nor encouraged by government or tourism boards. No travel commissions had mailed them pamphlets full of lies promising monster vegetables and a live-forever climate, bragging about gold mines, about grass so thick you could turn out your livestock and forget them. Some residents chafed at the baby boomers—their look, their work habits. They were vastly different from the well-scrubbed Colorado travelers of the 1950s, who'd come to Crested Butte by the dozens from cities like Denver, dressed like Roy Rogers and Dale Evans, hiring country musicians for dance parties at the local community hall. These newcomers were peaceniks and flower children and freaks. The vast majority were peaceful, though not all, as anyone who witnessed chairs being thrown through the front window of the Grubstake by recent arrival Trip Wheeler could attest. The marshal of Crested Butte would've leaned on this handful of ruffians a little harder, mind you, but at the time he was too young to go into the bars. Instead, when the patrons finally stumbled out in the wee hours at thirty below zero, as often as not he took them home and put them to bed. At the same time there were a few local bad boys more than happy to toss back a few whiskeys and beat up hippies. As well as one young rancher fond of shooting dogs running loose on his ranch on the outskirts of town, leaving his poor mother to comfort the owners—young hippie girls, mostly, standing on her stoop in peasant dresses with dead dogs in their arms, crying their eyes out.

All that aside, how any given town in the Rockies reacted to these strange-looking greenhorns depended greatly on the level of prosperity in the community at the time. Over the hill, in the more affluent village of Aspen, police magistrate and restaurant owner Guido Meyer was about as happy to see freaks on the street as he would've been to find Russians in the statehouse. Guido was surely the only man in America to have matchbooks for his restaurant printed that said "No Hippies" on the inside cover; it soon became sport for the freaks to sneak in when he wasn't

looking and try to grab a handful for souvenirs. One summer, having been greeted by a sign in the window of his
restaurant that said "No Beatniks Allowed," a large and
thoroughly motley crew of longhairs appeared on the streets
several days later, every one of them smiling peacefully and
wearing T-shirts that said "Eat at Guido's." Guido came
undone, ranting and raving, shaking his fists, swearing
revenge. In the end he was removed from the police force for
showing "substantial and enduring prejudice against defen-
dants in Municipal Court." Over in Crested Butte, meanwhile, economically speaking things were stagnant. Weary
miners were living in the shadows of worn-out diggings.
Ranchers were struggling to hold on. A dozen or so recluses
were there, too, fugitives from civilization who never really
meant to come here in the first place but, having done so,
couldn't think of much reason to leave. Houses could be had
for less than $10,000, and rooms went for a song. A Sneller's
Special Breakfast at the Forest Queen—one pancake, two
pieces of bacon, and coffee—could be had for a mere 79 cents.

Though Crested Butte had been a ski town since 1961,
it had little of the buzz and glitter of its more famous sister
on the other side of the Elk Mountains. ("At the time Aspen
was a little nuclear generator," explains one Crested Butte
resident, "throwing off realtors.") A lot of the young men
and women who came to the Butte did so on a budget. One
week they were counting out change for laundry in a tract
apartment in Biloxi or Daytona or New York, sleeping in a
crowded loft in L.A., and the next, by virtue of some rumor

being prattled by friends fresh off the road, they found themselves in the shadows of the Rockies, paying twenty-five bucks a month to live in Mrs. Yaklich's coal shed, surrounded by Croatian miners. It was those shared economic conditions that helped broker decent relations between most of the old-timers and the back-to-landers, bringing the groups together in ways that wouldn't have been possible in places on more solid financial footing. (Helen Hunt had written on the dicey economics of Crested Butte nearly a hundred years earlier, in an 1883 issue of the *Atlantic:* "Poverty Gulch and O-Be-Joyful Creek—they will always be found side by side, as they are in Gunnison County. Only a narrow divide separates them, and the man who spends his life seeking gold and silver is as likely to climb the wrong side as the right.")

While Guido was railing against the longhairs in Aspen, on any given summer afternoon in Crested Butte you could find hippie girls skinny-dipping at Nicholson Lake, waving and smiling at the contented old miners watching from their pickup trucks along the east side of the reservoir. Those same girls would later in the day gather in old Botsie Spritzer's living room, listening to stories, not to mention round after round of accordion music. The newcomers talked to the old boys about the past. They asked where to buy coal for their stoves, how to thaw pipes, what kinds of vegetables grow at 9,000 feet. And the answers were nearly always forthcoming. Dan Peha, stuck in Crested Butte in 1972 when the water pump on his old Dodge van gave out, said he knew he was home the moment he was hailed off the street by a group of complete strangers and invited to join a backyard barbecue hosted by a family of Croatian miners, complete with accordions and tambourines. "I thought it was so neat, here were these hippies and old-timers all mixed together; I'd never seen that before." Peha replaced the water pump, then stayed on in the Butte for another seven years.

For their part many of the newcomers tried to repay such kindness—helping old men saw wood, going around on winter mornings to rekindle the stoves of mining widows, even encouraging their fellow greenhorns to partake in local traditions. In 1968, for example, there appeared a good-natured editorial lauding the Slovenian Fourth of July celebrations, citing with enthusiasm how young Americans could learn a great deal from such traditions, pitying those "whose misfortune it has been to never hear an accordion in full heat."

And if such festivities were in short supply, there was always the chance to make something up out of what at least felt like traditional thread. Something people like editor George Sibley were only too happy to do. "If I was just going to report the news," he says, "it would've been a pretty freakin' boring newspaper. It dawned on me at the time that one of the best things about having a newspaper was the opportunity to invent things." Thus it happened that the one other feature on the front page of the *Chronicle* on the day of Bill Crank's mayoral victory was an announcement for

Flauschink Festival, "an ancient Yugo-Serbian festival marking the mythical marriage of winter and spring." In truth it had been created four years earlier, in a fortunate meeting at Frank and Gal's Bar between George Sibley, an unknown old man, and lots of beer. Especially telling is that a fair number of the old-timers joined in. On a certain spring day in the early 1970s you could've seen the mayor's wife, Sally Crank, being carted around in a convertible as Flauschink Queen, with seventy-something miner Pitsker Sporcich sitting beside her, having proudly assumed the mantle of Flauschink King.

Today George Sibley lives downstream, in Gunnison, and recalls the swell of newcomers to the Rockies in the 1960s and 1970s with a mix of fondness and regret. Through the 1960s and up until 1971 or 1972, he explains, the old-timers were pretty open to the people who came. They wanted the town to survive. "These were mostly either first- or second-generation people out of old Europe, where there'd been a strong sense of village feudalism. The way they survived the ravages of mining work and the mining economy here in Colorado was by keeping that sense of the village alive. They didn't retire and go to Arizona. They retired and went to Frank and Gal's Bar. They'd tell any story to anyone who wanted to listen, and were more than willing to listen back if they heard a good tale coming." George says that as the back-to-nature movement grew, it brought with it people who had no interest at all in the village concept. He and others were troubled by that—by the callousness, the indulgences. In his capacity as editor of the paper he started encouraging people to write a series called "Welcome Stranger, Don't Tread on the Town." "I was trying to get people to realize a little something about the place they were moving to. One old-timer told me he felt invisible to some of the newcomers. 'I feel like I'm just goddamn scenery around here. Nobody listens to anything we say; they think of us old-timers as just part of the woodwork.'"

Bill Crank says that when he ran for mayor he was concerned that he and his friends were taking the town away from the old-timers. "We were just a bunch of kids. Well, I was thirty-two, which made me far and away the oldest person on the council. From there the ages went down to like twenty-nine, twenty-eight, twenty-six, twenty-three, and twenty-one. If that happened today, I'd be thinking, Good God, what's going on here?" Crank, who recently retired from Crested Butte city government, says he understood well the apprehension of the old-timers, that this was an entirely different culture coming in. "They had a hard time understanding why, if everyone liked this town so much, and it was created and it evolved through mining over all those years, why mining was no longer good enough." (Though most of the existing mines had played out, newcomers were reluctant to encourage exploration for new lodes.) Then again, the very fact that people like George Sibley, Bill Crank, and a lot of others recognized this issue—that they understood mining not merely as exploitation but as the historical framework for an entire culture—put Crested Butte ahead of the curve.

Dan Peha, meanwhile, has a different notion of what strained the community, pegging the troubles to around 1975, when they paved Elk Avenue. "I really don't remember much in the way of animosity between the freaks and the old-timers. What I do recall is the real estate developers coming in, and their big thing was to pave Elk Avenue, which is the main downtown street. That's when I started noticing a split between the old-timers who wanted to keep things the way they were—and a lot of us newcomers stood with them, because none of us wanted to pay more taxes—and those who wanted to see the place developed. The freaks and the old-timers actually forced a vote on the issue. We lost, but it was close."

As the back-to-nature movement progressed it brought many who were looking less for a life than for a free-for-all. In a particularly inspired piece of writing in 1968, *Chronicle* editor George Sibley lambasted a group of newcomers making nuisances of themselves over in Aspen.

The problem children in Aspen, the problem children we will get here when they tire of Aspen, are no more flower children than were all the howling children of the past decade children of *Howl*. What they are in fact are the basically dull and unoriginal sons and daughters of basically dull and unoriginal mothers and fathers; they are the ones who tack onto any and every movement without understanding in the least what the movement is about. They are bored because they are too unimaginative to creatively amuse themselves, restless because they have energy they do not want to waste on work, stoned on drugs because they are tired of being stoned on the tube. They are not hip, they are not beat. They fight their nothingness by letting somebody else do the work of giving them their identity. Hopefully, when the tag-alongs come to Crested Butte, the townspeople will recognize them for what they are, and, sorting the wheat from the chaff and not throwing everything away just because it's the same color, will respect the good grains and dismiss the rest with the tolerant pity usually rendered to someone else's dull and spoiled child.

AT THE SAME TIME small towns in the Rockies were being populated by middle- and upper-middle-class white kids, they continued to be a refuge for another kind of person who'd been seeking out these mountains since the days of the fur trappers—those hiding from creditors, from the law, men and women escaping dead-end jobs or bad relationships. Plenty of Vietnam vets, too, having come to the wilds mostly to forget. The frontier West in general, and the Rockies in particular, had been touted throughout the nineteenth century as a critical relief valve for the nation, allowing the unemployed and other potential troublemakers to simply go away, break free from those good, stable citizens who were busy trying to advance the culture. When the FBI was canvassing the country in the late 1960s looking for certain members of the radical SDS and Weatherman underground groups, more than a few were hiding out here in the Rockies, in the faded Victorians and dilapidated shotgun houses of towns like Crested Butte.

Yet even among locals who were unhappy about the newcomers, it would've been inconceivable to turn in someone on the lam. There was yet alive in the Rockies, as there is to a degree even today, an old western commandment against asking questions about a person's past, reserving judgment instead for what he does in the present. Neil Murdock, who was arrested in late 2001 by the FBI for events stemming from a drug deal thirty years before, lived in Crested Butte for twenty years, with numerous people aware of his past, and by most definitions became somewhat of a model citizen. It was Neil who turned clunkers into mountain bikes, which he and a lot of others rode in a race to Aspen. It was Neil who helped start the day care center. Not surprisingly, when several years ago a knockoff of *America's Most Wanted* came with their cameras rolling, looking for him, no one in town would give them the time of day.

In wrestling with issues of development, tourism, and extractive industry—not to mention the rising cost of housing and various other economic forces—baby boomers in places like Crested Butte began building what some consider the roots of one of today's more intriguing schemes for community. Referred to as bioregionalism (a term first made popular by poet Gary Snyder), the philosophy advocates a brand of economics and government forged not along arbitrary political boundaries, but determined by natural ecosystem features and the human and nonhuman communities they contain. From a bioregional perspective the primary values of place aren't just property rights and development but the establishment of an economy based on sustaining both diverse human and biotic populations. In other words, one makes a choice to do something not based simply on the profits to be made but also on the effects such an action will have on both the culture that exists there and the ecosystem as a whole. Bioregionalism is a kind of regional populism, heavy on ecology, built around the belief that those who actually live in a particular system—people who know it intimately—are in the best position to figure out what uses are appropriate. In this sense it turns on an approach to life not unlike the one painted by Wendell Berry. "The right local questions and answers will be the right global ones," writes Berry. "The Amish question, 'What will this do for our community?' tends toward the right answer for the world." Whether a revolution in the making or another pipe dream, bioregionalism is among the first serious attempts to establish sustainable behaviors in a part of the country routinely plagued by anything but.

To the extent that there are visible roots to bioregionalism, they can be found in the 1960s back-to-the-land movement, perhaps especially as it played out in the American West. Far from being merely a fad, says Bron Taylor of the University of Wisconsin, the component of the counterculture such as that seen in Crested Butte "has greatly extended its influence." Many of those same people today, says Taylor, are arguing for bioregionalism as a moral imperative—a new kind of twist on traditional Enlightenment philosophy, if you will—which calls people to develop new sensitivities toward the places in which they live and work. Even if you view the effort as nothing more than poetry, even creative religious invention, the spirit of bioregionalism may in the end prove to be "a significant leap of human moral imagination."

All of which remains to be seen. But this much we can say for sure. The down-and-out old mining towns of the Rockies were in the 1960s raw canvas, as they'd been countless times before, destined to be splattered with quirky humor and political fervor, improvisation and arrogance, and every now and then with the kind of naïve, juvenile behavior that attends most bouts of cultural creativity. That was the gift of the region—to baby boomers, and to young people nearly a hundred years before, when various other black sheep found it a much needed antidote to mainstream culture. It was a place beyond convention. A land filled not so much with sacks of gold as with, better still, possibilities. The place where young girls of privilege could savor the smell of sagebrush and sweat. Where some fortunate black men managed to stumble through a rabbit hole and find themselves a million miles from slavery. Where sickly white men jumped into creeks and sucked at mountain air and sometimes grew strong again. Where Isabella Bird paused at 14,255 feet atop Longs Peak, finding at last the place where peace rested for one bright day.

CHAPTER 10

The Morning After

Mount of the Holy Cross

THOMAS MORAN

For some, this snow-filled couloir, located in Colorado's Sawatch Range, was proof of God's pleasure with our westering ways. Others, meanwhile, chose to see it simply as more proof that the Rockies were indeed the province of mysteries.

LONG BEFORE WALLACE STEGNER CAST HIS thin line of hope for Rocky Mountain society, anticipating the day the region would produce a class of "men to match the mountains," writer N. S. Shaler expressed similar thoughts in an 1881 article in the *Atlantic*. To Shaler the Rockies, "with all the features of this rather grim continent," possessed a kind of invincibility he was sure would remain undiminished "no matter how our fierce American life might beat upon their shoulders." Those living in the mountains, he suggested, would in time be shaped by the surrounding country, the strong nature of the land firmly stamping itself on the populace. Only then could we "expect to find the most distinctly American of our peoples—a race that will, we may hope, be cast in the large mould of the nature that surrounds it. The fierce, eager mood that is now upon this people will in time pass away, and they will lose their restlessness and gain strength in contact with the great strong land where their lot is cast."

Shaler was attempting to look beyond a region where the vast majority of people were transients—adventurers and holidaymakers, one writer put it—having come to play out their luck or engage in some sort of lark and drift away. As Rollin Hartt pointed out about Montana early in the twentieth century, relationships in that state remained mournfully fleeting. "You no sooner bind a man to you than forth he betakes him to Livingston, or Billings, or Glendive, or Missoula. The town is like an eddy in the river. The water runs into the eddy, the water runs out of the eddy; the eddy is always changing, yet the eddy remains unchanged. There is in Montana more opportunity for acquaintances and less opportunity for acquaintance than in any other part of the world." In the end Hartt resigned himself to the fact that the Rockies were merely an exaggeration of a universal law— that most of us go through the world in exactly this fashion, touching many hands, clasping few. "In time it is your turn to move away, east or west. You buy a ranching scene in water color by Charlie Russell, perhaps a mounted head from the taxidermist, a grizzly rug if you can afford it, a pretty handful of Montana sapphires (the blue are the loveliest of all). And you depart amid the cheers of your friends and admirers."

Yet while the transience Hartt and Shaler talk about was for the most part a choice, for an increasing number of today's residents it's a matter of necessity. As former Crested Butte mayor Bill Crank explains, long gone are the days of coming into a mountain town as a ski bum, working nights and weekends to buy a hopelessly run-down little fixer-upper and over the next half dozen years turn it into a home. You can still live with a bunch of people in a single house and play ski bum for a few seasons. But unless you have money, lots of it, sooner or later you're going to drift away. Writing in the *Mountain Gazette*, Cal Glover shares similar thoughts about Jackson Hole, where the average price of a two-bedroom house last year was a whopping $643,000— this in a depressed market. "I make four dollars and twenty-five cents an hour, so I'd have to work 151,294 hours, or 15,129 cab shifts . . . or about 210 seasons, to afford such a house. If I radiate enthusiasm and make a few tips, I could whittle that down to 105 years." Less than a third of the people who work in towns like Jackson, Steamboat, Vail, and Aspen can afford to actually live there. Of the wealthy who can afford it, many are no less fair-weather friends than those who roamed the Rockies a hundred years ago. One of the eeriest experiences in this region is to walk through entire subdivisions on a night in November or May, between ski season and summer holidays, and find there not a single lamp burning in the windows.

Wealth has brought other changes as well. One of the hottest new games among some well-off newcomers is "bagging touch-and-gos"—seeing how many backcountry airstrips you can touch with the wheels of your private plane in a given day without ever coming to a stop. At the northern edge of Greater Yellowstone work continues on the exclusive Yellowstone Club—a recreational hideout for the rich, with memberships going for $250,000 and annual dues of up to $16,000. Security is coordinated by former Secret Service agent Bruce Bales. In all it's a far cry from even forty years ago, when a handful of Hollywood stars were setting up homes in the remote valleys of Montana and Wyoming—not because such places were trendy, because they clearly weren't, but because such celebrities were desperate to hang out in a place where the neighbors weren't easily impressed. Today the famous have been joined by thousands of others who *are* impressed, and greatly so, fairly giddy with the thought of telling friends at cocktail parties in New York or Atlanta about their Wyoming ranch, just down the road from Harrison Ford.

Ironically, in some ways the environmental community itself helped foster such movement. Throughout the 1970s it was a common practice to argue locally for the preservation of untrammeled landscapes almost exclusively on the notion that such places would be highly sought after by a growing swarm of people who would pay handsomely for such backdrops. Beauty, then, far from being a basic human value—that agent of transformation celebrated by everyone from ancient storytellers to American landscape artists—became little more than cultural cachet. Lands that had long provided access to Freud's notion of healthy cultural fantasy—providing images not just of beauty but of danger and shadow—came to be thought of in terms of bistros, condos, and ski hills. In the 1890s Rudyard Kipling made a special point of describing a curious group of westerners he ran across as "so suffering from American materialism that they were inclined to sell off their abundant natural resources." These were people who "catered too willingly to the hordes of builders and tourists who swarmed like angry ants over sections of the region." But what in Kipling's time merited comment because it was somewhat of an anomaly has in our own time become common fare.

Ironically, even many of those who came to mountain towns during the back-to-the-land movement, going on to

eventually prosper themselves, these days show little toler-
ance for newcomers who look different, who are clearly outside the status quo. The mere placement of affordable
housing has become one of the most contentious planning
issues of mountain towns, as surrounding neighbors fret over
how it might diminish the value of their property. One can-
did old-time resident of Crested Butte—at one time a hippie girl herself—tells of recently making friends at an
exercise class with a young woman in her twenties, sporting
colored hair and tattoos up and down her arms. "My initial
reaction to her was really prejudiced. Then all of a sudden it
dawned on me: To what extent are those of us with money
likely to give a break to anyone who's different from us?"

If there's merit to the idea that human communities are
at least in part like natural ones, in the end weakened by
homogeneity, then the towns and rural valleys of the Rockies can be said to be losing vigor with every passing year.
Gentrification is tragic here for the same reasons it is everywhere. But somehow the losses can seem especially disap-
pointing—not merely on account of the obvious and rapid
destruction of nature (the loss of elk winter range to trophy
homes alone is staggering) but because the primary quality
of the Rockies was for 175 years as an alternative to conventional wealth and culture—again, as Remington put it, a
reminder of the life that exists "beyond tasseled loafers,
derby hats and mortgages bearing eight percent." Due in
part to a fortunate twist of rugged topography and disturbing weather, there have been well into recent times at least a

few folds, a nook here and a cranny there where the main-stream world hasn't necessarily gotten the upper hand. But they're disappearing fast. Unlike the remittance men of old, many of whom spent their funds acquiring the trappings of locals, today's wealthy newcomers are more likely to distin-guish themselves with the trappings of luxury.

EVERY BIT AS TROUBLING as gentrification, some might argue, is the fact that living in an increasingly virtual world has changed utterly our expectations of what the wild Rock-ies can provide. Rangers in the large wilderness parks of the range are ever more frustrated by visitors who have what some describe as "too much Disney in the blood." Indeed, policy advisers are especially concerned about the degree to which entertainment-based recreation is beginning to impact the management of wilderness preserves. "Take away the fear of consequences," says Dr. William Borrie of the University of Montana, commenting on Disney's con-structed, utterly benign version of nature, "and people let their guards down. The more the visitor perceives the land manager to be controlling things, the more they expect nature to be under the manager's responsibility." Biologists like Yellowstone National Park's Kerry Gunther are aston-ished by how disconnected visitors are from any sense of danger in the wild, citing how more and more people seem willing to approach within twenty yards of a grizzly bear for the chance at a good photo. Recently, when I suggested to a park visitor that placing her six-year-old son next to an enormous bull elk wasn't a good idea, especially during the rutting season, the woman grew incensed. "The Park Service wouldn't let these animals run around if they were dangerous!" she snapped. Meanwhile trailhead comment sheets at Yellowstone, Rocky Mountain, and Grand Teton National Parks contain ever more bizarre requests: *Build pens around some of the animals so we can see them better. Blast the rocks off the trail to make it easier to walk.*

The same illusions created for us at Disney World and Busch Gardens—nature fully childproofed, sweetened by predictability—are increasingly being applied to the last of the Rocky Mountain wilderness. These are the days of seasoned guides and outdoor leaders quitting the business by the dozen, saying how over the past decade more of their clients have become insolent, angry in the face of nothing more than the day turning cold and the sky sending rain. "Ten years ago trip marketing began gearing toward the Outdoor Material Culture," explains celebrated rafting guide Brad Dimmock. "Now it's the yup-scale deluxe cruise, the predictable and comfortable wilderness experience. Expectations mutated. Suddenly there were complaints, more trivial than you can imagine." Others talk of a growing trend in their clients to show up on the trail or the river with all the latest equipment—not so much for reasons of comfort or safety as because displaying the best gear is part of how they communicate their station in life, the power of their success.

At the same time, as Dr. Carl Mitchum at the University of Chicago writes, "Technology is increasing the knowability of wilderness. The sense of discovery and mystery, so much a part of the experience, is utterly lost." Helicopter rescue of hikers in the Rockies has gone up dramatically in the past decade—often arranged by the hikers themselves using cell phones, some telling frustrated rescue crews that rather than being injured, they were just "really tired." As James Gleick pointed out several years ago in his book *Faster,* the growing expectation to be in control, to be entertained, shows up in every corner of our lives. Park rangers talk about the modern visitor's amazing level of impatience when it comes to watching wildlife. "On the Discovery Channel," explains one Yellowstone naturalist, "you're guaranteed drama from the start of the show. Out here if people don't see that kind of action within five minutes of getting out of their cars, they either pack it up and head off to another location or drive over to the IMAX Theater in West Yellowstone and watch it on the big screen. I call it animal ADD." In short, over the past several decades we've come to expect from nature both predictability and immediate gratification—ironically, the two things people most often counted on the Rockies to keep in check. It becomes ever more difficult for us to see mountains the way Thomas Burnet saw them—as wellsprings of the pleasures that come when imagination expands in the presence of "wild, vast and undigested nature."

Yet on any given day, at least in the highest reaches of

the mountains, somehow the old dreams still seem close at hand. Here the world tosses back and forth between the opposing fantasies that energized the Rocky Mountain dreamscape for 150 years: the first being to transcend utterly the terror of nature, the second to become one with it. More than anything else, residents of the Rockies use this sublime grandeur as a balm for their concerns about gentrification, as a means of wrangling some small relief from hordes of visitors obsessed with ever more disconnected demands. Residents of Jackson, Wyoming, for example, facing more than three million tourists annually descending on their tiny town at the base of the Tetons, have for years been running off on nights and weekends to secret places tucked into the hills of the surrounding national forest.

Given this, it comes as no surprise that what's especially disquieting to many locals is a growing list of threats to the federal lands themselves. "Though a region of such natural beauty can never become the worthless desert described by Daniel Webster," declared *Time* magazine in 1980, "it can become so despoiled that life there is no longer very special." Today such threats are coming not from that small, militant gaggle of zealots who've been showing up regular as knapweed for seventy-five years, pushing to give the national forests "back to the states," ignoring altogether the fact that a key condition of statehood was to forgo any claim to federal lands. Such true believers, after all, claim only a small congregation (though one especially well funded by industry groups, including some with imaginative

names like Environmentalists for Jobs, organized in 1990 by
the president of the Chicago Mining Corporation). Far
more insidious is the steady dismantling of conservation
measures some fifty years in the making—efforts now being
led by the government itself, and for the most part outside
public scrutiny. Intoxicated by the work of economists like
Milton Friedman, whose religious-style belief in laissez-
faire capitalism was a major political force in the 1980s, a
powerful group of modern politicos is now intent on apply-
ing free-market principles to national forests and Bureau
of Land Management reserves across the length and breadth
of the Rockies. According to this vision—simple, elegant,
and, to some, utterly terrifying—the best use of any natural
resource is what the highest bidder will pay for it. If recreation or wildlife preservation cannot squeeze from the land
as many dollars as mining or logging can, then they shouldn't
be a management priority. Much of the ground for such
thought was established in the 1970s, when there was a
flurry of research by various universities to put dollar values
on every aspect of the out-of-doors; a day in the wilderness,
for example, was determined in one report to carry roughly
the same value as the price of a movie ticket. The problem
with such economic models—and, at the same time, what to
many is most appealing about them—is their utter lack of
dimension. The profit margins of many timber projects dry
up altogether when you factor in massive government subsi-
dies to build the necessary roads. Coal bed methane wells
are a bonanza only if you neglect to figure in the harm to

surrounding ranches and communities from potential damage to the aquifers.

Yet such projects may soon overwhelm the Rockies—arriving if not through the front door, then through the back. The recently launched Healthy Forest Initiative, for example, proposes to streamline certain logging projects—those meant to reduce the threat of wildfire—by restricting public and judicial input. Only then, promise those championing the legislation, can we finally overcome the massive "analysis paralysis" being caused by environmentalists, who they claim routinely tie up essential fuel reduction programs by appealing them in court. In truth, according to the Government Accounting Office, of more than 1,600 fuel reduction programs launched in 2001 and 2002, less than 2 percent failed to start on time. The fact that the government has no money to carry out such projects is to the free-market crowd a golden opportunity. Instead of using Forest Service crews, the Healthy Forest Initiative will outsource the work to private contractors. The only problem is that in order to be even marginally worthwhile to a contractor, a typical logging operation has to bring in substantially more profit than can be obtained from harvesting the kinds of relatively young, highly flammable trees that pose the highest fire risk. The solution will be to allow loggers to also take larger, more fire-resistant trees, which of course have far more commercial value. Thus in twenty to thirty years we may well have thousands of acres of even-aged timber stands, much of it lodgepole pine, which, beyond providing only marginal wildlife habitat, is arguably the most flammable forest of them all.

In similar fashion, after seven years' work and 1.6 million public comments—more than any other conservation project in history—the Roadless Area Review, which set aside millions of critical lands for wildlife, has been scrapped, with the government refusing to even defend it in court. As such protections are dismantled—a quiet process, often achieved by the stroke of a pen on a Friday evening before congressional recess—there is a growing queue of oil, gas, and coal bed methane developers eager to gain access to what some of the best biologists in America have pronounced critical wildlife habitat. Such wholesale development may well put various Rocky Mountain birds and mammals in a predicament biologists refer to as a mortality sink—a situation where species have suitable habitat for part of the year but perish due to a lack of feeding or breeding grounds needed to survive other seasons. Some argue for keeping numbers up artificially, such as by establishing more feeding areas for animals like the Rocky Mountain elk. The ethics of such schemes aside, nearly every ungulate disease—including one not unlike mad cow disease, known as chronic wasting—is far more easily communicated in such crowded conditions. Even though national parks are under siege by high-level government, proponents of free-market economics are arguing for the privatization of everything from naturalists to law enforcement rangers.

The very economic forces which throughout history

Americans felt needed to be moderated—preferably in places like the Rockies—now threaten to dismantle much of what made these mountains most unique. It's not that large numbers of people ever considered the region a serious alternative to capitalism; rather, the range provided for millions a precious respite from capitalism's incessant demands. Whether it was Teddy Roosevelt steeling his character with a hard ride across Montana or Margaret Andrews Allen smiling over poetical laundry days in the thermal basins of Yellowstone, something unique happened in these wild nooks and crannies. Even for those, as Henry George pointed out 125 years ago, "who have never thought of taking refuge upon it."

On our better days, as a culture we seem unwilling to give up entirely on the old notion that human personality is scoured and shaped, and ultimately made bright again, by the earth underfoot. That promise—though it may in one generation be slight, in another, brilliant—will no doubt continue to energize the struggle to imagine a richer, more layered vision of nature appropriate to modern times. Recreational development, as Aldo Leopold once wrote, is "a job not of building roads into lovely country, but of building receptivity into the still unlovely human mind."

In the meantime, winds continue to rage and blizzards howl. Stray thoughts come to rest on this peak or that, feast and grow strong, run down the mountains fast and free as wolves. By virtue of fortunate timing and timeless stature the Rockies have become the repository of a great many

uncommon perspectives about community, social convention, and greed. And while today it may seem that such
notions are dormant, if history is any teacher we might
expect them to rise again, tumbling cold and fresh across the
backbone of the continent.

Notes on Sources

FOLLOWING IS A SMALL SAMPLING of the resources used to write *The Great Divide*, many of which may be of value to those exploring the cultural and natural history of the Rocky Mountains. A wealth of historical information in particular can be found at various archives and special collections around the country; among the most notable are Yale University's Beinecke Library, the University of Wyoming's American Heritage Center, the Denver Public Library, Yellowstone National Park Archives, and the Huntington Library in San Marino, California.

INTRODUCTION

Rocky Mountain Reader. Ray Benedict West, editor (Dutton, 1946)

Virgin Land: The American West as Symbol and Myth. Henry Nash Smith (Harvard University Press, 1950)

Account of an Expedition from Pittsburgh to the Rocky Mountains in the Years 1819 and *'20.* Dr. Edwin James

Under Western Skies: Nature and History in the American West. Donald Worster (Oxford University Press, 1922)

The Legacy of Conquest: The Unbroken Past of the American West. Patricia Nelson Limerick (W. W. Norton, 1987)

Something in the Soil: Legacies and Reckonings in the New West. Patricia Nelson Limerick (W. W. Norton, 2002)

The Life Story of a Great Indian: Plenty-Coups, Chief of the Crows.
Frank Linderman (1930)

A Lady's Life in the Rocky Mountains. Isabella Bird (G. P. Putnam's
Sons, 1881)

CHAPTER ONE: FIRE, ICE, AND A HUMORLESS GOD

Land Above the Trees. Ann H. Zwinger and Beatrice E. Willard
(Harper & Row, 1972)

*The Sacred Theory of the Earth: Containing an Account of the Original of the Earth, and of All the General Changes Which It Hath
Already Undergone, or Is to Undergo, till the Consummation of All
Things.* Thomas Burnet (R. Norton, 1681)

Mountain Gloom and Mountain Glory: The Development of the Aesthetics of the Infinite. Marjorie Hope Nicolson (Cornell University Press, 1959)

The Green Man: The Archetype of Our Oneness with the Earth.
William Anderson (HarperSanFrancisco, 1991)

*Paleoenvironmental History of the Rocky Mountain Region During
the Last 20,000 Years.* Cathy Whitlock, University of Oregon,
Mel A. Reasoner, University of Colorado, Carl H. Key, U.S.
Geological Survey Biological Resources Division (1998)

Postglacial Vegetation and Climate of Grand Teton and Southern Yellowstone National Parks. Cathy Whitlock (Ecological Society of
America, 1993)

Climatic Changes Since the Last Glacial Maximum. H. E. Wright Jr.
et al., editors (University of Minnesota Press, 1993)

"Freshwater Forcing of Abrupt Climate Change During the Last
Glaciation." Peter U. Clark, Shawn J. Marshall, et al. (*Science,*
July 13, 2001)

"Future Climate in the Yellowstone National Park Region and Its Potential Impact on Vegetation." P. J. Bartlein, C. Whitlock, and S. L. Shafer (*Conservation Biology,* 1997)

CHAPTER TWO: THE RISE OF
THE MOUNTAIN MAN

A Life Wild and Perilous: Mountain Men and the Paths to the Pacific. Robert M. Utley (Henry Holt, 1997)

The Oregon Trail. Francis Parkman (Little, Brown, 1894)

A Short Detail of Life and Incidents of my trip in & through the Rockey Mountains. James Clyman (State Historical Society of Wisconsin, 1871)

"Life in the Rocky Mountains: A Diary of Wanderings on the sources of the Rivers Missouri, Columbia, and Colorado from February, 1830, to November, 1835." W. A. Ferris (*Western Literary Messenger,* 1842–44)

Rocky Mountain life; or, Startling scenes and perilous adventures in the Far West during an expedition of three years . . . Rufus B. Sage (Thayer and Eldridge, 1859)

Rocky Mountain Rendezvous: A History of the Fur Trade Rendezvous, 1825–1840. Fred Gowans (Brigham Young University Press, 1975)

Journal of a Trapper. Osborne Russell (Syms-York, 1914)

The River of the West. Mrs. Frances A. Fuller (R. W. Bliss, 1870)

The Mountain Men and the Fur Trade of the Far West. Leroy Hafen, editor (Arthur H. Clark, 1965–72)

The City of the Saints, and Across the Rocky Mountains to California. Richard F. Burton (Harper & Brothers, 1862)

Journal of an Exploring Tour Beyond the Rocky Mountains. Samuel Parker (Mack, Andrus and Woodruff, 1842)

"Marriage and Settlement Patterns of Rocky Mountain Trappers and Traders." William R. Swagerty (*Western Historical Quarterly,* 1980)

Probing the American West. Ray Billington, editor (Museum of New Mexico Press, 1962)

A Preliminary Bibliography on the American Fur Trade. Compiled by John Ewers and Stuart Cuthbertson (Martino Publishing, 2002)

Narrative of the adventures of Zenas Leonard, a native of Clearfield county, Pa., who spent five years in trapping for furs, trading with the Indians, &c., &c., of the Rocky mountains. Zenas Leonard (D. W. Moore, 1839)

The Journals of Lewis and Clark. Bernard De Voto, editor (Houghton Mifflin, 1953)

A number of articles and editorials concerning the Hayden expeditions appeared in the *New York Times,* each offering important clues about nineteenth-century attitudes toward science and the West. Noteworthy issues include:

1871: September 18
1873: August 7, 18; September 7
1874: April 16; November 3, 16, and 26; December 12
1875: January 18; April 27; July 2; August 29 and 31; September 19

CHAPTER THREE: A FAITH MOVED BY MOUNTAINS

Kit Carson's Life and Adventures: The Nestor of the Rocky Mountains, from Facts Narrated by Himself. De Witt Peters (W. R. C. Clark, 1858)

Kit Carson: Pioneer of the West. John S. C. Abbott (Dodd and Mead, 1873)

Domestic Manners of the Americans. Frances Trollope (G. Routledge, 1839)

History of the city of Memphis and Shelby County, Tennessee. J. M. Keating (D. Mason, 1888)

"The Montanians." Rollin Lynde Hartt (*Atlantic,* June 1898)

"Nature and Democracy." Peggy Wayburn (article in *Wilderness and the Quality of Life,* edited by Maxine McCloskey and James Gilligan [Sierra Club Books, 1919])

CHAPTER FOUR: SLOW AND RESTLESS, REVENGEFUL AND FOND OF WAR

Of Plymouth Plantation: The Journal of William Bradford. William Bradford (1630–47)

New English Canaan. Thomas Morton (Amsterdam, 1637)

The Switzerland of America: A summer vacation in the parks and mountains of Colorado. Samuel Bowles (American News Company, 1869)

A Biobibliography of Native American Writers, 1772–1924. Daniel F. Littlefield and James W. Parins, editors (Scarecrow, 1981)

A Journey to the Rocky Mountains in the Year 1939. Dr. F. A. Wislizenus (Rio Grande Press, 1969)

"Manifest Destiny in the West." Mrs. F. F. Victor (*Overland Monthly,* August 1869)

"An Indian Girl's Story of a Trading Expedition to the Southwest About 1841." Winona Adams, editor (*Frontier,* May 1930)

CHAPTER FIVE: LORDS, FARMERS, AND OTHER TOURISTS

The Backwoodsman; or, Life on the Indian Frontier. Friedrich Armand Strubberg and Sir C. F. Lascelles Wraxall, editors (John Maxwell, 1864)

Edward Warren. Sir William Drummond Stewart (G. Walker, 1854)

"Prairie and Mountain Life—1843." Clyde H. and Mae Reed Porter, editors (unpublished ms., University of Wyoming American Heritage Center)

"Moccasin Trail." Mae Reed Porter (unpublished ms., University of Wyoming American Heritage Center)

Journal of M. A. Cruikshank (Yellowstone National Park Archives, 1883)

"Beyond the Legend of Colter's Hell: The Early Exploration of Yellowstone National Park." Merrill J. Mattes (*Mississippi Valley Historical Review,* September 1949)

"Yellowstone Park." A. B. Guptill (*Outing,* July 1890)

"A Family Camp in Yellowstone Park." Margaret Andrews Allen (*Outing,* November 1885)

Journal of Katherine Stephen (Montana Historical Society Archives)

CHAPTER SIX: PREACHERS WITH PAINTBRUSHES

"Essay on American Scenery." Thomas Cole (*American Monthly,* January 1836)

Notes on the State of Virginia. Thomas Jefferson (1785)

Nature's Nation. Perry Miller (Harvard University Press, 1967)

New Lands, New Men. William Goetzmann (Viking Penguin, 1986)

"Landscape in America." Mary Gay Humphreys (*Art Journal,* January 1888)

"The Inalienable Land: American Wilderness as Sacred Symbol." William E. Grant (*Journal of American Culture,* 1994)

"The Tree and the Stump: Hieroglyphics of the Sacred Forest." Robert L. McGrath (*Journal of Forest History,* April 1989)

"Rocky Mountains." Letter from Albert Bierstadt (*Crayon,* July 10, 1859)

"Letters on Landscape Painting." A. B. Durand (*Crayon,* January 1855)

Discovered Lands, Invented Pasts: Transforming Visions of the American West. Jules David Brown, Nancy K. Anderson, et al. (Yale University Press, 1992)

The Rocky Mountains: A Vision for Artists in the Nineteenth Century. Patricia Trenton and Peter Hassrick (University of Oklahoma Press, 1983)

CHAPTER SEVEN: A MONACO GAMBLING ROOM IN A COLORADO SPRUCE CLEARING

Dude ranch brochures, correspondence from Montana Historical Society

The Rockies. David Lavender (Bison Books, 1981)

"To Leadville." Helen Hunt (*Atlantic,* May 1879)

Journal of Joseph Warren Arnold. American Heritage Collection, University of Wyoming Special Collections

Rocky Mountain West: Colorado, Wyoming, and Montana, 1859–1915. Duane A. Smith (University of New Mexico Press, 1992)

The Dome of the Continent. Colvan Verplanck (*Harper's New Monthly Magazine,* December 1872)

The Yellowstone Story. Aubrey Haines (Yellowstone Library and Museum Association, 1977)

"The Wild Parks and Reservations of the West." John Muir (*Atlantic,* January 1898)

"The Yellowstone National Park." John Muir (*Atlantic,* April 1898)

Medical Geography in Historical Perspective. Nicolaas A. Rupke, editor (Wellcome Trust Centre for the History of Medicine at UCL, 2000)

"Aspects of American Life." Charles Dudley Warner (*Atlantic,* January 1879)

Through Glacier Park: Seeing America First. Mary Roberts Rinehart (Houghton Mifflin, 1916)

Fatal Environment: The Myth of the Frontier in the Age of Industrialization. Richard Slotkin (Atheneum Publishers, 1985)

CHAPTER EIGHT: THE COMING OF THE DUDES

Dude Ranching: A Complete History. Lawrence R. Borne (University of New Mexico Press, 1983)

"Recapturing the West." Jerome Rodnitzky (*Arizona and the West: A Quarterly Journal of History,* 1968)

"The Origins and Early Development of Dude Ranching in Wyoming." Charles G. Roundy (*Annals of Wyoming,* 1973)

Dressing the Dude. staff written (*Vogue,* May 1936)

Journals of Joseph Warren Arnold. American Heritage Collection, University of Wyoming Special Collections

"Ernest Thompson Seton as Artist and Naturalist." R. L. Duffus (*New York Times,* November 17, 1940)

The Nature Fakers: Wildlife, Science and Sentiment. Ralph Lutts (University of Virginia Press, 1990)

"Woodcraft Extolled as the Science That Makes Men." Ernest Thompson Seton (*Current Opinion,* October 1922)

A Woman Tenderfoot. Grace Gallatin Seton-Thompson (George N. Morang, 1900)

CHAPTER NINE: SEASON OF THE FREAKS

"Oh-Be-Joyful Creek and Poverty Gulch." Helen Hunt (*Atlantic,* December 1883)

"Field Observations: An Interview with Wendell Berry." Jordan Fisher-Smith (*Orion,* Autumn 1993)

"Disneyland and Disney World: Constructing the Environment, Designing the Visitor Experience." William T. Borrie (*Loisir et Société* [Society and Leisure], 1999)

"Wilderness in the 21st Century: Are There Technical Solutions to Our Technical Solutions?" Wayne Freimund and Bill Borrie (*International Journal of Wilderness,* 1997)

"Bioregionalism: An Ethics of Loyalty to Place." Bron Taylor (*Landscape Journal,* 2000)

CHAPTER TEN: THE MORNING AFTER

"A Winter Journey Through Colorado." N. S. Shaler (*Atlantic,* 1881)

"Roads and Their Major Ecological Effects." Richard T. Foreman and Lauren E. Alexander (Harvard Graduate School of Design, 1998)

Photograph Credits

Chapter 5: *Stewart's Camp, Lake, Wind River Mountains* (1865)
Alfred Jacob Miller
The Maryland Historical Society, Baltimore, Maryland

Chapter 6: *Alice's Adventures in the New Wonderland, the Yellowstone National Park* (1885)
Courtesy The Toppan Rare Books Library (F722.N67), American Heritage Center, University of Wyoming

Chapter 7: *Buffalo Bill Cody's Wild West Show Brochure* (1911)
Buffalo Bill Historical Center, Cody, Wyoming; MS6.6A.1.1

Chapter 8: *Valley Ranch Brochure*
Buffalo Bill Historical Center, Cody, Wyoming; MS14.2C.1/3

Chapter 9: *Hippies on the Company Store Bench* (1970s)
Photo by Sandra Cortner

Chapter 10: *Mount of the Holy Cross*
Thomas Moran
Denver Public Library, Western History Collection, T-97

Index

Page numbers in *italics* refer to illustrations.